Fifty Days for Soaring Vision

A FIFTY-DAY DEVOTIONAL FOR A FOUNDATION BUILT ON SOLID BIBLICAL PRINCIPLES

Rick Joyner

MorningStar Publications

A DIVISION OF MORNINGSTAR FELLOWSHIP CHURCH

P.O. Box 440
Wilkesboro, NC 28697

Fifty Days for a Soaring Vision
Copyright © 2001 by Rick Joyner
Third Printing, 2005

Distributed by MorningStar Publications, Inc., a division of MorningStar Fellowship Church,
375 Star Light Drive, Fort Mill, SC 29715

International Standard Book Number: 1-929371-05-5

MorningStar's website: www.morningstarministries.org
For information call 1-800-542-0278.

Cover Design: Micah Davis
Book Layout: Dana Zondory

Table of Contents

Introduction

The purpose of this devotional is to impart a clear and practical vision of our inheritance in Christ. When the Lord called Abraham, one of the first things that He did was give him a vision of what he was to inherit, as we see in Genesis 13:14-15:

> And the LORD said to Abram, after Lot had separated from him, "Now lift up your eyes and look from the place where you are, northward and southward and eastward and westward;
> for all the land which you see, I will give it to you and to your descendants forever."

After the Lord showed Abraham his inheritance, He then commanded him to: **"Arise, walk about the land through its length and breadth; for I will give it to you" (Genesis 13:17).** Likewise, after we receive a vision of our inheritance, we must begin to walk in it. That is why our vision must be practical. We must walk in what we see.

It is crucial for every Christian to know how far they can go in Christ, where they are at the present time, and what is the next step along the way. As Paul wrote in Ephesians 3:17, we must be **"rooted and grounded in love"** to be able to comprehend the extent of our inheritance. Love is the foundation of true Christian character. This devotional seeks to build vision day by day so we can comprehend the inheritance we have in Christ, while at the same time fortifying our basic Christian character, which is defined as **"the fruit of the Spirit" (Galatians 5:22).**

As I have sought to interweave vision and character, there is some intended repetition, reminding, and reviewing included. These are for the purpose of building a bridge to new insights, but also because repetition greatly increases retention. This is often not considered good literary style, but my goal is not to be literary. My goal is to see the church become the bride that she is called to be for the King of kings. In all of my writing I seek to plant seeds and water them so that we can bear fruit that will remain.

If you have read ***Fifty Days for a Firm Foundation,*** you will see that this book takes many of the great biblical truths that are established in it and carries them further and higher. However, as we go further and higher we need to do so from a strong foundation. Even though it is not essential to have read the first ***Fifty Days*** devotional to benefit from this one, it would be helpful.

As you read this over the next fifty days, my prayer for you is found in Ephesians 3:16-21:

> **that He would grant you, according to the riches of His glory, to be strengthened with power through His Spirit in the inner man;**
>
> **so that Christ may dwell in your hearts through faith; and that you, being rooted and grounded in love,**
>
> **may be able to comprehend with all the saints what is the breadth and length and height and depth,**
>
> **and to know the love of Christ which surpasses knowledge, that you may be filled up to all the fulness of God.**
>
> **Now to Him who is able to do exceeding abundantly beyond all that we ask or think, according to the power that works within us,**
>
> **to Him be the glory in the church and in Christ Jesus to all generations forever and ever. Amen.**

DAY 1

A Noble Faith

It was said of the Bereans, **"Now these were more noble-minded than those in Thessalonica, for they received the word with great eagerness, examining the Scriptures daily, to see whether these things were so" (Acts 17:11).** It is right to listen to new things with openness and eagerness. We are an old wineskin if we are not open to that which is new. However, as eager as we should be for the Lord's new wine, we must always take what we hear to the Scriptures to verify it.

Most Christians know what they believe, but few seem to know why they believe it. We are each responsible for establishing the truths upon which we believe for a solid biblical foundation. Without this, regardless of how accurate what we believe is, the foundation of our faith will be weak. Even the Son of God responded with **"it is written" (Matthew 4:4),** when tempted by the devil. Even the Word Himself based His doctrines and actions on the written Word. How much more should we?

If you see some people digging a footing, you know that a house or small building will be going up. However, when you walk downtown and see an entire block fenced off, and you see that beyond the fence a deep hole is being dug, you know that something of significance is being built there. We too must dig down before we build up if we want our lives to be significant. We must establish for ourselves every truth that we believe, or we will be limited in how much we can be used in this life. The more effort we put into the foundation of our spiritual lives, the more that can be built upon them.

The church is about to enter some of its most challenging times, so that it can then enter into its most fruitful times. The darkness is gathering, but so is the light. Every challenge to our faith is allowed by God to strengthen our faith. Trials always strengthen true believers and remove those who are pretenders. There is a great pruning coming so that those who are truly abiding in the Vine can bear more fruit.

When a tree is pruned, the branches removed are the ones that are just making more wood and not bearing fruit. Are our lives bearing fruit for the kingdom, or are we just producing more wood, hay, and stubble? If we are not growing in fruitfulness we are in danger of being pruned. The only way we can be fruitful is to be properly joined to the Vine. In our study of the Scriptures, we must seek to be more closely united with Him. As the Word Himself said in John 5:39-40:

"You search the Scriptures, because you think that in them you have eternal life; and it is these that bear witness of Me;

and you are unwilling to come to Me, that you may have life.

We receive life by coming to Him. The life that is on a solid foundation is not just one that understands doctrine accurately, but is one that is joined to the Word, Himself. It is not just knowing the Book of the Lord, but knowing the Lord of the Book. However, because He is Truth, we must love the truth and be passionately devoted to accuracy of doctrine as well.

The Holy Spirit is moving upon the hearts of Christians everywhere to sink their roots deeper into the written Word. A deep passion for the Scriptures is spreading over the church. It will bring forth a love for truth and righteousness that will begin to radically affect congregations everywhere. This is a holy leaven. If just one or two in a congregation catch this passion, it will spread to all.

As our foundations become stronger, they will enable the Lord to give us more power and more spiritual authority. However, let us always remember that we seek truth in order to live it, not just know it. Jesus was full of **"grace and truth" (John 1:14)**. Truth without grace brings a form of godliness that has no power. Love changes truth into grace that gives life. We must seek truth because we love the truth and want to be united with the One who is the Truth.

We must not seek to love so that we can be trusted with power, but power is a means by which God expresses His love. Love is always the goal, not the means. As we read in I Timothy 1:5: **"But the goal of our instruction is love from a pure heart and a good conscience and a sincere faith."** Therefore, let us do all that we do out of love. Let us search the Scriptures because we love them, we love the truth, we love the One whose truth it is, and we love the people He gave His life to save.

DAY 2

Who Can Discern Truth?

As we pursue sinking our roots deeper into God's Word, we need to understand the basic biblical principles that lead to truth, and most of all, lead to Him who is the Truth. A fundamental requirement for discerning the truth is found in the remarkable statement made by the Lord in Matthew 11:25:

> **At that time Jesus answered and said, "I praise Thee, O Father, Lord of heaven and earth, that Thou didst hide these things from the wise and intelligent and didst reveal them to babes."**

As the Lord Jesus Himself declared, the immature are far more likely to have a greater understanding of the Scriptures than the wise and intelligent. Most of the great perversions of Scripture have come from those who believed that they had a superior insight into the Scriptures because of their wisdom and intelligence. Does this mean that we should seek to stay spiritually immature? Of course not. However, we must understand that true spiritual maturity has qualities that are childlike. The Lord also said in Matthew 18:3:

> **"Truly I say to you, unless you are converted and become like children, you shall not enter the kingdom of heaven."**

A child is teachable. Being teachable is one of the basic qualities of humility. In James 4:6 we are told: **"But He gives a greater grace. Therefore it says, 'God is opposed to the proud, but gives grace to the humble.'"** God's ways are much higher than our ways. In order for us to understand Him or His Word, we must keep a humble, teachable attitude.

In Scripture, the Word of God is called a river of life. A river is ever-flowing, continually going somewhere. If we remain in that river, we, too, will be ever-flowing, and moving forward. As we are told in I Corinthians 2:10: **"For to us God revealed them through the Spirit; for the Spirit searches all things, even the depths of God."** If we are following the Spirit, we will be going deeper. Even the knowledge of basic doctrines will be expanding for us as we come to understand the depth of His ways. However, they should never expand beyond what can clearly be established by the Scriptures themselves. In all things we must always come back to **"It is written" (Matthew 4:4).**

DAY 3

The Sum is Truth

In John 10:35 Jesus said, **"...the Scripture cannot be broken."** None of God's truths are isolated, they are all interrelated and do not stand alone. As Psalm 119:160 states it: **"The *SUM* of Thy word is truth."** All of Scripture fits together in the most intricate, beautiful, harmonious pattern, just like the balance of nature in the creation. Balance is an important word if we are to understand and walk in biblical truth.

An article I once read stated that if the earth deviated from its orbit around the sun just the equivalent of one eighth of an inch over a one hundred mile distance, we would either freeze or fry. The forces which keep us in such a tiny little slice of space that supports life are the gravitational pull of the other planets, our moon, and the earth's "wobble" on its axis. If any of these forces were changed, we would have a catastrophic deviation from our orbit. In a similar way we, too, must be in a right relationship to the foundational biblical truths. The "spiritual gravitational pulls" of these truths on our lives will keep us in the right "orbit" that supports true life.

There are foundational doctrines of the faith that we must keep in harmony and balance if we are going to stay on track. These basic doctrines of the faith cannot be compromised or changed. They should each have their proper influence to keep us in the right place. In Hebrews 6:1-2 we are given these basic truths:

> **Therefore leaving the elementary teaching about the Christ, let us press on to maturity, not laying again a foundation of repentance from dead works and of faith toward God,**
> **of instruction about washings, and laying on of hands, and the resurrection of the dead, and eternal judgment.**

The basic teachings are: 1) Christ, 2) repentance, 3) faith, 4) sanctification (instruction about washings), 5) spiritual authority (laying on of hands), 6) the resurrection, and 7) judgment. All of these together provide the proper "gravitational pull" in our spiritual lives to keep us in the proper orbit so that we continue to abide in true spiritual life.

The earth's "wobble" on its axis provides for the changing of the seasons. If it were not for the seasons on earth, the ice would form only on one side causing the earth to wobble out of its proper orbit. Likewise, we too may have seasons in our lives when certain truths are emphasized. We need to continually flow from one to the other just like the natural seasons. This helps to keep us in balance so that we do not wobble out of the path in which we have been called to walk.

As great as each of these foundational truths are, the over-emphasis of any one of them to the exclusion of the others will throw us off of the path of life. For example, a strong foundation of repentance is essential for a healthy spiritual life. However, if it is not also balanced with a strong understanding of faith, it will lead to the black hole of self-centeredness. Likewise, we need to have a good understanding of God's judgment, but it must be balanced with an understanding of the resurrection. All of these truths are meant to have a "gravitational pull" on our lives, but they must be kept in balance with each other so that none of them overly dominates.

Hebrews 6:1 begins by encouraging us to "leave the elementary teaching about the Christ" so that we can press on to maturity. We must understand that this is not an encouragement to leave the teachings about Christ, but only the elementary ones about Him. As we press on to maturity our knowledge of Him should be continually increasing. However, we do not need to continue in just the elementary teachings about Him, we must go on to the deeper ones.

Spiritual maturity is described in Ephesians 4:14-15:

As a result, we are no longer to be children, tossed here and there by waves, and carried about by every wind of doctrine, by the trickery of men, by craftiness in deceitful scheming;

but speaking the truth in love, we are to grow up in all aspects into Him, who is the head, even Christ.

The more any plant grows, the farther its branches will grow from the roots. Even so, it is a strong connection to those roots that allow the branches to keep growing. We are called to be **"oaks of righteousness" (Isaiah 61:3).** It is said of oaks that their root system is equal in size and span to the branches. What you see above the ground is matched by what is under the surface. If we want to be a great planting of the Lord, we must give as much attention to developing our hidden spiritual lives with the Lord as we do to any outward ministry. Sadly, studies have shown that the average pastor spends less than five minutes a day in prayer. Could this kind of shallow root system be why so many large ministries are so easily toppled?

DAY 4

Maturity Leads
to Unity

Though every believer should be rooted in all of the basic Christian doctrines, no one person, church, or movement has all the truth. As we discussed earlier, the gravitational pull of all the different planets help keep the earth in its proper orbit. Likewise, all the spiritual heavenly bodies need each other's influence to stay in their proper orbits. What we have must be joined to what the Lord gives to the rest of His body if we are to have the whole truth. This is stated in the Lord's Prayer the night before He was crucified:

> **"And the glory which Thou hast given Me I have given to them; that they may be one, just as We are one;**
> **I in them and Thou in Me, that they may be *perfected in unity*, that the world may know that Thou didst send Me, and didst love them, even as Thou didst love Me" (John 17:22-23).**

The Greek word that is translated **"perfected"** in this Scripture could have been translated "completed." Either way, the Lord has established that the only way we can fulfill our purpose is to be properly joined to the whole body of Christ. This is why Paul did not write that "I have the mind of Christ," but rather **"...*we* have the mind of Christ" (I Corinthians 2:16).** No one person or one body of believers can contain His mind. It takes the coming together of the whole body for us to have His mind.

Because of this, when the church comes into this unity, the world will know that He was indeed sent from the Father. We will not be able to come into such a unity without Him, so when we do we will both perceive and reveal Him. However, we will not come into this unity by seeking unity, but only by seeking Him. Unity as a goal in itself can be a false god—a stumbling block to both the mind of Christ and true unity.

True unity will never be built on compromise or political alliances, but rather on the revelation of the Son of God as the only Head of His church. Revelation is a *revealing* from God. The revealing from God is always the Son. When the Lamb comes in, even the twenty-four elders will cast their crowns before His throne (see Revelation 4:10). Who could ever presume glory or position in His Presence? When He is revealed, all the things that now divide us from one another will seem just as petty and profane as they are.

When we see the love that He has, we will be ashamed of our lack of love for Him and one another. Our crowns will also come off as we humble ourselves before His great glory. Then we will not be seeking position or recognition, but we will be consumed with a passion to see His glory revealed. That passion to see the Son of God exalted is from the Holy Spirit. Jesus is the Truth, and Jesus is Reality. All other endeavors will pale when He is revealed, just as the stars fade when the sun rises. This is the glory that He prayed for us to have so that we could be perfected in unity—it is the glory that He had with the Father in the beginning. This is why John wrote:

but if we walk in the light as He Himself is in the light, we have fellowship with one another, and the blood of Jesus His Son cleanses us from all sin (I John 1:7).

When we walk in the light of the Son, we will have fellowship with one another, and we will be cleansed of all unrighteousness by His life (blood) that flows through us. As blood can only flow through those members that are joined to the body, we, too, must be joined to His whole body if His life is to flow through us.

DAY 5

The Burnt Stones

The Books of Ezra and Nehemiah are two of the most important prophetic messages for our times. They contain the story of how a remnant of God's people returned to Jerusalem from captivity in Babylon to rebuild the temple of the Lord and the walls of the city. These faithful ones met with continuous opposition and criticism from the nations around them, and even from some of their own fellow Jews who had remained in the land. One of their most vehement enemies, Sanballat, said the following concerning them:

And he spoke in the presence of his brothers and the wealthy men of Samaria and said, "What are these feeble Jews doing? Are they going to restore it for themselves? Can they offer sacrifices? Can they finish in a day? Can they revive the stones from the dusty rubble even the burned ones?" (Nehemiah 4:2)

Today the enemy of the work of God is making the same railing accusations. There is a remnant of people who are leaving the comfort of religious Babylon with a vision of seeing the temple of the Lord restored to its former glory. It takes extraordinary faith to leave Babylon and make the spiritual journey to the place where the temple is going to be rebuilt, and where there will be a true church life just as the Lord intended it to be from the beginning. Then, after the journey has been made, we can expect the attacks from the jealous critics and enemies of the Lord to be continuous. One of the challenges that can be counted on is the question raised above: How can these be rebuilt with burnt stones?

In fact, both the rebuilt temple and walls of the city were constructed with stones that had been burnt during the destruction of the former temple and city. These were the ones that had been through the previous failure and now looked useless for building anything, much less the glorious temple of the Lord or the walls that represented salvation (see Isaiah 60:18). Are you one of these burnt stones? Have you been through a work that seemed glorious and pregnant with potential, only to end in a terrible disappointment? Have you been burned? If so, then you are a prime candidate for the glorious new work that the Lord is doing today.

Burnt stones may not look good on the outside, but they have been through the fire—they have been tested. It takes a great faith to endure a tragic failure, and then rise up again with a determination to keep pursuing the vision. Think of the kind of faith that it took for this remnant to return to the scene of their greatest failure and devastation with the resolve to start all over again. It takes that kind of vision to endure the opposition and discouragements that will surely come during the restoration.

If you have not been through the testing of a serious spiritual failure, you may be too idealistic to understand the real purpose of what the Lord is doing. Everything that the Lord is doing in this age is intended to be a testimony of His power of redemption. As stated, burnt stones may not look as good on the outside, but the Lord has never cared about what His dwelling places looked like on the outside. Those who have been through the fire of failure and are ready to be used again are probably just right on the inside for what He wants to build.

Both Ezra and Nehemiah ultimately prevailed because they kept their focus on the work and refused to let the criticism or opposition stop them. They did answer their accusers at times. They worked with their swords in one hand and were always ready to do battle if attacked. We will have to learn to do the same. There will be times to work and fight, but let us always remember that our main job is to complete the work.

We all come for the same thing, to see the Lord have a habitation among His people. To have His manifest Presence in our midst is worth anything that we must endure. Those who are called to the work must learn to recognize those that Jude called **"faultfinders" (Jude 1:16 NIV)** and resist them. It is part of the testing that must come with every significant work.

Such attacks also tend to thin the ranks of those without the courage to be part of the work at this stage. When Israel mustered for battle, the Lord often removed those who were too fearful from the ranks. This is a pruning that must take place before something of true spiritual significance can be built or before some important battles can be fought. Criticism and false accusations really should be encouraging to us. There are times to answer them, and there are times to draw the sword against the accuser of the brethren, but most of the time we just need to keep our attention on the work that we have been given to do. The greatest answer to every criticism will be the completed work.

DAY 6

Vision With Power

Dietrich Bonhoeffer is one of my favorite authors. He was a true prophetic voice during the first part of this century. He stood against the greatest darkness of his time without compromise and died because of it in a Nazi concentration camp. In one of his books, *Life Together*, he made a bold and shocking remark, stating simply: "God hates the visionary." The translation from the German language in which he wrote this may be a little stronger than he intended, but there is some truth to this that we should understand.

Vision is a powerful force. Almost all human advancement is the result of someone having a vision. It has been a great encouragement for me to see so many with a vision gather in our local congregations. I have listened to many visions, and I feel that most of them really are from the Lord. It has stirred me with the knowledge that there is a potential for something even more extraordinary than I could have even hoped for just a couple of years ago. However, if we are going to fulfill our callings as individuals and as a church, we must now go beyond just having a vision.

Almost everyone, Christians and non-Christians, have a vision of what they want to do or be, and yet very few fulfill it. Vision alone has never accomplished anything. Between the place of having a vision and seeing it fulfilled, there is always a lot of hard, tedious work that few visionaries have been willing to do. I think that was the source of Bonhoeffer's frustration with visionaries.

That is why, regardless of how good a person's vision sounds, I cannot get too encouraged about it until I see him or her also having a heart to work. Having the vision is the fun part. Walking it out will usually be much more difficult. Between the place where we receive the promise and the Promised Land, there will be a wilderness that is the opposite of what we have been promised. That wilderness is where our faith in God is purified, and our knowledge of ourselves becomes much more realistic. The wilderness is the place where the mere visionaries are separated from those who have true faith, and who love the purposes of God enough to pay the price to see the visions fulfilled. That is why James wrote: **"For just as the body without the spirit is dead, so also faith without works is dead" (James 2:26).**

God did not call us out of bondage just to wander aimlessly in the wilderness. He called us to walk in the full inheritance that He gained for us on the cross. We cannot settle for anything less. It is time to get through the wilderness and start possessing the promises that we have been called to inherit. When I see so many with great visions, but also great hearts and a willingness to work, it convinces me that this is the time to cross over. However, let us not forget that even after we have crossed our Jordan River and have begun to eat the fruit of the land, the battles will have just begun. Possessing our promises will be hard, but it will be worth it.

We must combine vision with the wisdom to know how to do the work, the faith to know that it can be done, along with the resolve to actually do it. As we studied yesterday, those who have a vision to see the house of the Lord restored and the walls of His great city rebuilt, will suffer attacks from within and without. However, those with true faith will not be deterred. Our goal is to hear on that most glorious judgment day, **"Well done, good and faithful servant. (Matthew 25:21 NKJV)** You finished the job I gave you to do."

DAY 7

Visions With Values

Today it seems as if those who have the most rock solid values are lacking in vision. Likewise, many who have vision are lacking in values. It must be our goal to have vision with values. We want to sink our roots deeper and deeper into sound biblical truth with a genuine commitment to the moral standards and integrity that are clearly mandated by Scripture.

For an effective vision, we also need to increase our perspective of history. We will accomplish very little that is truly new and fresh if we have to "re-invent the wheel" over and over. It is from the firm foundation of rock solid values, combined with the wisdom and humility to receive from those who have gone before us, that we can look into the future and prepare for what is to come. True vision has strong roots.

When we are talking about the "new" thing that is coming, we are not just talking about re-engineering the church. A fad of re-engineering swept through western industry over the last couple of decades, and it is now sweeping much of the church. Most of this was needed in industry and the church. But we need to be delivered from the four walls of the church and our "meeting mentality," and see the church become a living, vibrant force that functions twenty-four hours a day, seven days a week. However, just like much of the devotion to re-engineering in industry only resulted in some being able to make the wrong products better, many in the church have thought that by adopting a new methodology they could become more relevant to the times. New methodologies can be helpful, but we need more than that. The very definition of Christianity needs transforming.

To many Christians, faith is but an appendage to their life, rather than the essence of life itself. Jesus did not come to die on the cross so that He could meet with us a couple of times a week. He came to be our life. This is our ultimate calling and purpose—for Jesus to be our life so we can manifest the life and power that is found in Him. This will never be done because we have better buildings or better programs. Our labor is for Christ to be formed *in* His people. Our goal is to try to present every man complete in Christ.

This is not a new message. In fact, there have probably been some who have preached it in every generation. Even so, to actually do it would be radical indeed, which must be our goal. We must consciously live and move and have our being in Him (see Acts 17:28). Our ultimate goal should be to only think thoughts that He would think, to only say what He would say, and to do what we see Him doing. This is our calling as ambassadors of the King—to represent Him by having Him live His life through us.

I have watched our local prophetic ministry teams in amazement. These people are really hearing from God, and they are being used to radically impact thousands of lives. I feel that their gifts are constantly going to new levels. However, we are feeling more acutely aware of the need for those with gifts of interpretation. Most who get the higher levels of revelation do not have the gift of interpretation. Now we are trying to team those with obvious gifts of interpretation with those who get revelation.

True prophetic interpretation does not come from just knowing biblical symbolism. Interpretation is a prophetic gift in its own right. It is interesting that the two men who probably had the greatest gifts of interpretation in Scripture, Joseph and Daniel, only seemed able to interpret dreams that came to others. They actually could not interpret the revelation that came directly to them. The Lord seems intent on making us need others regardless of how great our gifts are.

Even when we have revelation and interpretation, there is yet another phase, which is *application*. This is not so much a prophetic gift as it is a realm of wisdom given mostly to the apostles, pastors, and teachers. We have had quite a few prophetic words that we felt compelled to send out which resulted in calls from pastors asking what they should do in response to these words. Often our response was, "We don't know. That's your part." This usually shocked them, but we know our limits and how much we need them to get the full picture.

Even the greatest prophetic ministry will only see in part. Therefore, to understand the entire picture we must put what they get together with what others are seeing. There are many immature, impatient, or idealistic people that believe if someone is really hearing from God they should get the whole message. But that is a presumption which causes many of the problems people have with the prophetic.

The best only see in part, so whenever we hear a prophetic word, we need to keep seeking the Lord for the other parts. The Lord has composed His body and distributed all of the gifts so that we need each other. No one can stand alone without the rest of the church. Therefore, we will not have an accurate vision unless we are properly joined to the entire body of Christ.

Our own local church has seen much growth in the prophetic gifts. We believe we will one day have hundreds of mature prophetic ministries of New Testament stature sent out from our church. We also know that our future contribution to the church is going to require that all of these be joined with the present evangelistic, pastoral, and teaching ministries to help prepare the way for the coming apostolic ministry.

It will be a glorious day when all of the ministries that the Lord has given to His church are able to function together in unity. That is the Lord's plan for the perfection of His people (see John 17:23). Even so, it is only as we keep our attention on the ultimate purpose of God that we will be safe from making idols out of His lesser purposes. The ultimate purposes of God are not just having ministries walk in unity with each other, but having all of His people in unity with Him.

These times are pregnant with potential. The windows of heaven seem to be continually open. We can all go as high as we desire, and as far as we have the faith to go. As Paul Cain once said, "We are all as close to God as we want to be." The veil has been rent, and the door is open. Let's take advantage of the great blessing we have been given to live in these extraordinary times with the knowledge we have been given by the Truth, Himself. Let's not keep waiting for someone to come stir the waters while the King Himself is standing right next to us! It is time to go ahead and step out of the boat and walk with Him.

It is time to go for the highest vision of all, being like Him and doing the works that He did. Being like Him means that we must be deeply and completely devoted to the values of the Lord. This was first of all love—love for Him and love for one another. It is right to be devoted to the gifts of the Spirit because the Scripture commands us to **"earnestly desire" (I Corinthians 12:31)** them. However, all of the gifts work through faith, and faith works by love. We should esteem the gifts of the Spirit, but from the most solid foundation of devotion to the fruit of the Spirit.

DAY 8

Getting Out of the Wilderness

A couple of years ago I was complaining in my heart about the obstacles that we had encountered in several areas of our ministry that were slowing down our progress. As I was sitting in my chair thinking about what I could do to get these things moving faster, the phone rang. It was my prophetic friend, Bob Jones, and he started talking as if he had been listening to my thoughts.

Bob began with, "You're sitting there impatient, wondering what you can do to get things going, but the Lord is the One who slowed you down." He went on to encourage me that we are on time, and we will accomplish what He has called us to do. He also said that we still do not have the complete plan, or God's timing on everything, so we needed to keep seeking Him.

Almost ten years ago Bob had given me a word that we were to assemble a certain number of people in Charlotte. When these were assembled, the Lord would add a zero to our number, quickly multiplying our number by ten times. He also said that the key word here is "assembled," which means much more than just gathering people for meetings. It means to be put together, like one would assemble a puzzle.

We have several times the number of people meeting than the original number we were given, but probably less than half of that number know their place in the body, and even less than that have actually begun to function in their place. Though progress is being made, we still do not have the required number "assembled."

I was also told that another reason why the Lord had slowed us down was because there was grumbling and complaining in the camp. What shocked me was that I was one of the guilty ones, as I was actually complaining in my heart when Bob called. We are told in the book of Hebrews that grumbling and complaining was a primary reason why the first generation of Israel was not allowed to enter the Promised Land. Complaining will keep us from the promises of God, which is also one of the reasons why many have not yet been released into their callings.

In whatever we are complaining about, we are really complaining about the Lord. If we complain about the leadership over us at our jobs, we are complaining about the Lord's leadership in our lives, because He obviously put them there (see Romans 13). If we are complaining about our spouse, parents, children, or any other circumstances, we are complaining about the way the Lord is ordering our lives. It takes faith to please God and to move Him, and complaining is the opposite of faith. Complaining does not start things moving—it stops them. Complaining can be one of the most powerful enemies keeping us from walking in His purpose for our lives.

I was also told that during this time of being put in the Lord's holding pattern, we were going to be tried by depression. For someone like me, waiting is one of the most depressing things there is. I also know that many in our congregation have already spent years waiting on God, so just the mention of having to wait longer will be understandably difficult. Even so, if we give into depression or doubt it will cause us to stay in the wilderness even longer. Depression is sin because whatever is not of faith is sin, and depression does not embrace faith. It takes faith to inherit the promises of God.

There are some chemical and biological problems that can cause depression, but most of the depression we suffer from has a spiritual root. A victory over every spiritual stronghold was gained for us at the cross. We must not be satisfied with anything less than a complete victory over depression, and determine that we are going to view every situation with faith, not doubt. If we are getting tired of the wilderness, it is time to review the promises of God and encourage ourselves in His faithfulness.

Depression basically comes from seeing our situation from the dark side. This happens whenever we stop looking through the eyes of faith. It was depression that caused ten of the twelve spies who were sent to look over the Promised Land to come back with an **"evil report" (Numbers 13:32 KJV).** It is interesting that their report of the land was true and was basically the same report given by the two faithful spies, Joshua and Caleb. However, the ten saw the obstacles as being too great for them to overcome, while Joshua and Caleb believed they could overcome since God was on their side. In both cases it was not *what* they saw that differed, but *how* they saw them.

Like the first generation of Israel to come out of Egypt, many Christians never walk in the promises of God to which they are called because they fall into grumbling and complaining. Sadly, many succumb to this just before they are about to be released from the wilderness. Having been there so long, the temptation to doubt was the greatest then. The fastest way out of the wilderness is to be thankful, even for the wilderness. We enter the Lord's gates with thanksgiving and His courts with praise (see Psalm 100:4). Let's determine that we are going to abide in Him in every area of our lives, and we can do that by being thankful for everything.

I was told by the word that came through Bob that our unbelief and complaining had put us in a holding pattern for one year. Now it seems that everything is moving at a pace that is hard to keep up with. It is now hard for me not to long for the time we were in the holding pattern! The apostle Paul said that he learned the secret of being content regardless of whether he was abased or abounding (see Philippians 4:12). We must do the same. Let's determine to grow in faith, not doubt. The demonstration of faith is faithfulness. Let's war against any tendency to complain about anyone or anything, and in all things give thanks. Let's enter His gates with thanksgiving and His courts with praise and stay there.

DAY 9

The Power of Purpose

A recent study made by Richard Leider and David Shapiro found that the number one fear that people have is to live a meaningless life. Finding one's purpose and fulfilling it is the deepest yearning of the human heart, even more compelling than fame or fortune.

Those who have had the most clearly defined purposes have been the leaders of the world. As Laurie Beth Jones stated in her book, *The Path:* "People with a clearly defined mission have always led those who do not have one. You are either living your mission or you are living someone else's."

One of our primary purposes at MorningStar is to help people find their purpose in God. Every Christian has a high calling to be like the Lord, to do the works that He did, and to represent Him to this world. Because of this high calling, everything that a Christian does can have eternal significance for those around them. What could be more important than that?

"Many are called, but few are chosen" (Matthew 22:14). This means that many come to know their callings, but few go on to fulfill them. Many are called to do great things, but they do not fulfill that calling because they do not give themselves to the little things. If we are not faithful in the little things, we will not fulfill our purposes in life. Martin Luther King, Jr. once said: "If you are a street sweeper, determine that you are going to be the best street sweeper who ever lived. Sweep streets like Michelangelo painted. If you become the best street sweeper who ever lived, the world will beat a path to your door to see the best street sweeper who ever lived."

The first step toward fulfilling our purposes is to understand that there are no insignificant tasks. The people who become the greatest at great things are also usually great at everything they do. Those who do great things have greatness in them, not just in their tasks. If you will do whatever you are doing now with all of your heart as unto the Lord, and if you will face every task with that passion and a devotion to excellence that His work deserves, you will do great things because greatness will be in you. Remember, you were made in the image of God who does all things well.

I have been privileged to know some of the most successful people in the fields of business, sports, entertainment, government, the military, and ministry. I have observed success from many vantage points. The reasons for success are the same in every case, and they are strikingly simple. Leo Tolstoy, possibly the greatest writer who ever lived, started one of his classics with an insight that applies here: "Every happy family is alike. Every unhappy family is unhappy in its own way." The secret to success in almost any field is the same, and it is easy to understand. Failure is much more complicated.

The principles for success are basic and simple. If you try to make them more complicated than they are, you will fall into the traps that keep people from their purpose. As Paul wrote to the Corinthians,

But I am afraid, lest as the serpent deceived Eve by his crafti- ness, your minds should be led astray from the simplicity and purity of devotion to Christ (II Corinthians 11:3).

The shortest route to knowing your purpose and fulfilling it is to do all that you are given to do with all of your heart, as unto the Lord. Whatever you have now been given to do, do it like Michelangelo painted. The world may or may not ever take note of it, but the Lord will. He will trust you with even more talents if you treasure and use well the ones He has already given to you.

DAY 10

Know Those Who Labor Among You

If we are going to be successful in a major endeavor we must learn one of the most powerful skills that anyone can have—team building. One of the Lord's highest priorities when He walked the earth was to build His team. He gathered a core of future leaders who had to be joined to Him and to one another. This is still one of His highest priorities in building His church and therefore must be ours.

There are few truly great teams that can be built quickly. Certainly the Lord was the best who ever was or will be at this. It took Him over three years to build His disciples into the team that would lay the foundation for His church. Of course, His church is to be His eternal bride and such a lasting purpose demanded the most painstaking care in laying the foundation. Teams for short-term missions may be put together much faster. Even so, the greatness of our work on any level will be significantly affected by our skill as a team builder.

We have a goal in our local churches to see every man, woman, and child know their place in the body and be equipped to function in it. We are doing this because the Word of God is clear that the New Testament ministry is given **"for the equipping of the saints for the work of service, to the building up of the body of Christ; until we all attain to the unity of the faith, and of the knowledge of the Son of God, to a mature man, to the measure of the stature which belongs to the fulness of Christ" (Ephesians 4:12-13).** Here it says clearly that these equipping ministries are given **"until we all attain...the measure of the stature which belongs to the fulness of Christ."** Is there anywhere on earth that a church has attained to that? Therefore, we must still give ourselves to the equipping of the people, but always keep in mind that our ultimate goal is to see all grow up into **"the measure of the stature which belongs to the fulness of Christ."** Teams are not an end in themselves, but an essential means.

As Ephesians 4 reveals, all New Testament ministry is meant to be a part of a team. All of these equipping ministries must function together for the proper equipping of the people. For these ministries to function together they must know each other. Then the team must go on to do as Proverbs 27:23 states, **"Know well the condition of your flocks, and pay attention to your herds."**

This may seem elementary because the larger the flock, the more difficult it is to know the individual sheep very well. The larger the flock, the more important it is for the ministry to work together as a team and for those within the congregation to be equipped to become a part of the team.

Hebrews 13:17 states that those who serve as leaders must keep watch over the souls of the people as those who will give an account. These are the Lord's own people whom we have been given to watch over and serve. The greater number of people that we have been given authority or influence over, the more we are going to need help. Therefore, our goal must be to see each one that we have the responsibility to watch over become strong enough to be able to watch over others.

When the Lord gave His messages to the seven churches in Revelation, He ended each one with a call to the overcomers, which is the calling of every Christian. True church life is meant to be on three levels: our individual relationships with the Lord, as families, and as a congregation. We must be overcomers in each area. Together these make a cord of three strands that is not easily broken (see Ecclesiastes 4:12). Therefore, as we are exhorted:

> **Let love of the brethren continue.**
>
> **Do not neglect to show hospitality to strangers, for by this some have entertained angels without knowing it.**
>
> **Remember the prisoners, as though in prison with them, and those who are ill-treated, since you yourselves also are in the body.**
>
> **Let marriage be held in honor among all, and let the marriage bed be undefiled; for fornicators and adulterers God will judge.**
>
> **Let your character be free from the love of money, being content with what you have; for He Himself has said, "I will never desert you, nor will I ever forsake you,"**
>
> **so that we confidently say, "The Lord is my helper, I will not be afraid. What shall man do to me?"**
>
> **Remember those who led you, who spoke the word of God to you; and considering the result of their conduct, imitate their faith.**

Jesus Christ is the same yesterday and today, yes and forever.

Do not be carried away by varied and strange teachings; for it is good for the heart to be strengthened by grace, not by foods, through which those who were thus occupied were not benefited.

We have an altar, from which those who serve the tabernacle have no right to eat.

For the bodies of those animals whose blood is brought into the holy place by the high priest as an offering for sin, are burned outside the camp.

Therefore Jesus also, that He might sanctify the people through His own blood, suffered outside the gate.

Hence, let us go out to Him outside the camp, bearing His reproach.

For here we do not have a lasting city, but we are seeking the city which is to come.

Through Him then, let us continually offer up a sacrifice of praise to God, that is, the fruit of lips that give thanks to His name.

And do not neglect doing good and sharing; for with such sacrifices God is pleased.

Obey your leaders, and submit to them for they keep watch over your souls, as those who will give an account. Let them do this with joy and not with grief, for this would be unprofitable for you.

Pray for us, for we are sure that we have a good conscience, desiring to conduct ourselves honorably in all things.

And I urge you all the more to do this, that I may be restored to you the sooner.

Now the God of peace, who brought up from the dead the great Shepherd of the sheep through the blood of the eternal covenant, even Jesus our Lord,

equip you in every good thing to do His will, working in us that which is pleasing in His sight, through Jesus Christ, to whom be the glory forever and ever. Amen (Hebrews 13:1- 21).

DAY 11

Breakthrough in
the Air

Robin McMillan once told me that he could "smell a breakthrough." I thought that was a funny way to put it, but I had to admit that I could too. It was as if there was a special energy in the air, and you could actually smell a coming release in the Spirit. For about a year we had been in a holding pattern with many of our projects, and sure enough soon after Robin and I had this conversation, there seemed to be a breakthrough on every front.

Of course, when you are advancing, it is important that you not take more land than you can hold. I was recently in a meeting with the head of the largest bank in America. He told us how they had been asked by the government to provide about five hundred million dollars for inner city projects. This was to enable those who had successful small businesses in the inner cities to expand them. However, the result was that all of this money ended up hurting these small businesses more than helping them. By giving them so much money, they were able to take a huge leap in size, but these people were not given the training on how to run a large business. Many of those who were successful on one level went bankrupt on the next level because they were given resources for which they were not ready. Has this not also been the reason for the failure of many churches and ministries?

It is good to have a big vision, but many who are vision driven are prone to take on responsibilities for which they are not yet prepared. There is an old saying: "Any job can be accomplished if it is broken down into small enough steps." Having a clear vision of our ultimate purpose is good, but if we are overly focused on the ultimate purpose rather than the next step, it is likely that we are going to be stumbling over some things. It was for this reason that the Lord made Israel conquer their Promised Land one battle at a time. He told them that He was not going to let them do it too quickly because the beasts of the field would take it over (see Exodus 23:29). He did not want them to conquer land until they were strong enough to hold it. The same is true with us.

The most encouraging thing to me about what is happening at our local congregations is that many of the spiritual exploits are not coming through the full-time leaders, but through individuals and small groups who are hearing the Lord's voice and responding. Every week I hear of remarkable things that are happening completely without orchestration from our office. The church office is not supposed to be the head of the church, but Jesus is. To me this is real Christianity, with the Lord moving through the different members of the body as it pleases Him. As we read yesterday from Ephesians 4:12-13, let's look at the next couple of verses.

but speaking the truth in love, we are to grow up in all aspects into Him, who is the head, even Christ,

from whom the whole body, being fitted and held together by that which every joint supplies, according to the proper working of each individual part, causes the growth of the body for the building up of itself in love (Ephesians 4:15-16).

One of the main things that the Lord is doing now is forming the "joints." A joint is not a part, but it is where two parts come together. This will ultimately enable the **"proper working of each individual part."** This has to happen for many to go to the next level of their vision. Just as Barnabas had to go get Paul before he could be released in his own ultimate calling, there are joinings that must take place between the members of the body before we can all go to the next level. The Lord has so composed His body that we all need each other, and none of us are going to get there alone.

DAY 12

The Path of Wisdom

Wisdom is the ability to apply knowledge properly. In Proverbs 24:3-4 we are told: **"By wisdom a house is built, and by understanding it is established; and by knowledge the rooms are filled with all precious and pleasant riches."** It is true that sermons filled with knowledge will tend to draw people. The gift of a word of knowledge will also draw crowds. This is good, but our purpose in the Lord is not just to draw crowds, but also to see people built together into the house of the Lord. To do this we need wisdom. The gift of a word of wisdom may not be as spectacular as the gift of a word of knowledge, but it is every bit as essential for the work of God to be accomplished.

The following are just a few of the Scriptures that exhort us about the value and advantages of wisdom.

> **For wisdom is better than jewels; and all desirable things can not compare with her (Proverbs 8:11).**

> **How much better it is to get wisdom than gold! And to get understanding is to be chosen above silver (Proverbs 16:16).**

> **Wisdom strengthens a wise man more than ten rulers who are in a city (Ecclesiastes 7:19).**

> **Wisdom is better than strength (Ecclesiastes 9:16).**

> **Wisdom is better than weapons of war (Ecclesiastes 9:18).**

How do we acquire wisdom? We just need to ask as we are told in James 1:5. **"But if any of you lacks wisdom, let him ask of God, who gives to all men generously and without reproach, and it will be given to him."** It is wisdom to understand that we need wisdom. This is a fundamental humility, which is a prerequisite for wisdom. As we read in Proverbs 11:2, **"When pride comes, then comes dishonor, but with the humble is wisdom."**

A basic characteristic of humility is teachableness. A tragic pride has gripped our soul when others cannot teach us. The depth of our humility might be demonstrated by how open we are to being taught by those who might be considered inferior. Was this not the great test and the reason why the Lord, who was Wisdom Himself, came as a humble carpenter? Is this not why He called the **"uneducated and untrained" (Acts 4:13)** to be His apostles? It seems that He so structured His ministry and His church to filter out the proud and attract only the humble. We can see that this is basic to the Lord's nature in both James 4:6 and I Peter 5:5 which states that **"God is opposed to the proud, but gives grace to the humble."**

Knowledge fills our lives, but wisdom builds them. Therefore, in the building of our lives, families, churches, and ministries, the seeking of wisdom must be a priority. To do this we must seek humility. It is therefore wisdom to associate with the lowly, and learn to patiently listen to those who we may be prone to think are inferior. As the Lord Jesus Himself rejoiced, saying, **"I praise Thee, O Father, Lord of heaven and earth, that Thou didst hide these things from the** (worldly) **wise and intelligent and didst reveal them to babes" (Matthew 11:25).** He also said that we would have to become like little children to enter the kingdom (see Matthew 18:3). One of the basic characteristics of children is that they are teachable. Humility is the way the kingdom will come to our lives.

DAY 13

Knowing the Path

The basic purpose of every Christian is to become like the Lord and to do the works that He did. We do this by loving Him and our neighbors. Everything we are called to do will fit in one of these categories: loving God or people. We may distinguish the path on which God has called us to walk by determining the path that compels us to walk in love.

If we truly love the Lord, we will love what He loves and hate what He hates. Proverbs 6:16-19 declares:

> **There are six things which the LORD hates, yes, seven which are an abomination to Him:**
> **Haughty eyes, a lying tongue, and hands that shed innocent blood,**
> **A heart that devises wicked plans, feet that run rapidly to evil,**
> **A false witness who utters lies, and one who spreads strife among brothers.**

Because these are the things that the Lord hates, we can immediately know that anything which falls into any of these categories will be evil. If we love the Lord we will not do them.

The first thing that He hates is **"haughty eyes."** This is pride that is manifested by the way we look at others or ourselves. If we begin to look down on other churches or ministries because we think that ours is superior, are we not guilty of this? If we have been positioned a little higher than others for a time, it is for the purpose of service, not exaltation. Therefore, we should consider those who may not be as "exalted" as we are as the ones we are called to serve.

The next thing that the Lord hates is **"a lying tongue."** He is the Truth and those who love Him will love truth. The devil is the **"father of lies" (John 8:44)**, and we must consider all lies as the devil's work.

The next thing that the Lord hates is the shedding of **"innocent blood."** This is closely linked to lying in John 8:44, which we also need to consider was spoken by the Lord to the most religious people of His day:

You are of your father the devil, and you want to do the desires of your father. He was a murderer from the beginning, and does not stand in the truth, because there is no truth in him. Whenever he speaks a lie, he speaks from his own nature; for he is a liar, and the father of lies (John 8:44).

We see here that the devil murdered when he did not stand in the truth. Did he not use lies to deceive in the garden, and through those lies release all of the death that the world has known? Lies lead to death. Lies can be more deadly than bullets or bombs.

The next thing that the Lord hates is **"a heart that devises wicked plans."** Remember that one of the first things said about the serpent in the garden, which was a personification of the devil, was that he was **"crafty" (Genesis 3:1).** Craftiness implies devising plans to bend or break the rules and get away with it. This is a manifestation of the lawlessness that is the basic nature of the "man of sin," or "antichrist." We must learn to recognize the crafty for what they are, and repent of craftiness when it arises in our own hearts.

The next thing that the Lord hates is **"feet that run rapidly to evil."** Is there something in us that is drawn to evil? Is there something that derives a satisfaction, even an excitement, when we hear about acts of evil or violence? This is a manifestation of the base, fallen nature that has led to much of the suffering that mankind has endured. The Lord hates it and so should we.

It is also interesting here that the Lord hates feet that run **"rapidly"** to evil. I have learned that whenever I was pressured into doing something fast, it turned out to be a mistake. The faster I was pressured into going, the worse mistake it was. Carl Jung once said, "Hurry is not *of* the devil, it *is* the devil."

The next thing that the Lord hates is **"a false witness who utters lies."** This is the root of slander, gossip, and backbiting that divides the church the Lord died to save and unify. This can lead to becoming a stumbling block, the very last thing that the Lord said we should ever want to be. If we even pass on slander and gossip, we are just as guilty as the one who originated it. Therefore, we should be quick to recognize it and refuse to participate in it, knowing it is something that the Lord hates.

The last thing listed as something that the Lord hates is **"one who spreads strife among brothers."** This is to be distinguished from those who slander and gossip because they can use truth to spread strife and division. This is how the devil, who is called **"the accuser of our brethren" (Revelation 12:10),** comes as an **"angel of light" (II Corinthians 11:14),** or "messenger of truth." We can share absolute truth, but share it incompletely or even in a tone that brings division and strife. We must always remember that the Lord has given us a **"ministry of reconciliation" (II Corinthians 5:18),** and He hates the things that we do that cause division.

Remember our basic calling is to love the Lord and to love our neighbors. Let us judge everything that we do by the love standard. Are we doing it out of love for the Lord and His people? If we love the Lord, we will also love the truth because He is Truth. If we are abiding in Him, we will always use truth in love.

DAY 14

The Reward of Confidence

Hebrews 10:35 states, **"Therefore, do not throw away your confidence, which has a great reward."** In every sphere of life, *confidence* can be a primary factor that makes the difference between victory or defeat. Successful sports teams will quickly tell what a significant part confidence played in their victories. Successful generals will often point to the confidence they had in their troops as a reason for military victory. Victorious troops will usually point to the confidence they had in their generals. Successful businessmen will usually point to the confidence they have in their people or products as the reason for their success. The reward of confidence is success.

More than any other people on earth, Christians should go through life with confidence. We have the best Leader. There is nothing that the world could ever produce more valuable than the gospel that we have been given, and He is making His people into the greatest souls who ever walked the earth.

Yet many Christians still live their lives in fear, timidity, and defeat. Regardless of who you are, or your present circumstances, if you are a Christian this can and must change. Not only can you have victory, but overwhelming victory in every area of your life. This does not mean that your life will be without trials. In fact, victory is the consequence of one thing—battle! However, Christians are to live as **"more than conquerors" (Romans 8:37 KJV).**

A conqueror is one who is actually looking for battles in order to take more territory. That should be the mentality of every Christian— we should always be looking for a fight against the evil spiritual strongholds that are hindering our own lives, and then against the ones that are hindering others. That is why Christians are often referred to as an "army." We have been called to battle. Every trial or battle that we have in life is an opportunity to fight the good fight of faith, but only those with confidence will see them as such.

Confidence is a powerful word, and biblical confidence is a powerful force. Some of the most important biblical teachings center around this word. Confidence is the key to perceiving the will and victory God has for us. Paul said, **"Overwhelming victory is ours through Christ, who loved us enough to die for us" (Romans 8:37 LB).** This verse reflects the depth and power of a conviction that was the foundation of the apostle's life. Despite distress, persecution, tribulation, famine, nakedness, peril, and sword, Paul lived above it all as more than a conqueror. We too can live as more than conquerors because Jesus conquered and spoiled Satan at Calvary (see Colossians 2:15). Living according to the power of this great truth is the power to live an overcoming life. The victory of the cross is the source of our confidence, and if we live by it we will always eventually see triumph.

DAY 15

Ascending on the Path of Life

> **Good and upright is the LORD; therefore He instructs sinners in the way.**
>
> **He leads the humble in justice, and He teaches the humble His way (Psalm 25:8-9).**

It takes humility to know God's ways. The Lord teaches **"the humble His ways"** because one must be willing to learn in order to be taught. As we covered previously, one definition of humility could be *teachableness*. To be open and able to learn is one of the most valuable characteristics that anyone can have.

In this text, right after we are told that the Lord will teach the humble His way, the next verse gives us one of the most basic insights into the Lord's ways:

> **All the paths of the LORD are lovingkindness and truth to those who keep His covenant and His testimonies (Psalm 25:10).**

If we will stay on the Lord's paths, we can know that those paths will be lovingkindness and truth. If you are ever in doubt as to the way of the Lord, then choose the way of mercy and truth. There are limits to the Lord's mercy, which if reached will result in judgment. However, throughout the Scriptures we see that the Lord is usually far more merciful than His people tend to be. Therefore, we have this warning and this hope from James 2:13:

> **For judgment will be merciless to one who has shown no mercy; mercy triumphs over judgment.**

We are also told in Galatians 6:7, **"Do not be deceived, God is not mocked; for whatever a man sows, this he will also reap."** Therefore, if we want to receive mercy, we should learn to sow mercy every opportunity that we get.

Just as the President gives out pardons every New Year, the Lord will freely pass out pardons to all who ask and to all who trust in His mercy because of the cross. We can start all over again, erasing every failure and mistake. This is one of the greatest benefits of Christianity which has no match in any other religion or philosophy on earth. However, we are also instructed that if we are walking in **"His way"** we will also freely pass out pardons to those whom we might be able to hold something against.

It takes humility to ask for forgiveness, which is to acknowledge our sin. It takes the knowledge of the Lord's ways and a union of our heart with them to forgive others. However, if we are going to remain on the path of life, these are fundamental. So let us give mercy just as it has been freely given to us. One of the greatest freedoms we can ever have is when we know that we have been forgiven our sins. The second greatest freedom that we can ever know is when we forgive others.

The paths of the Lord are always ascending, carrying us higher and higher into the Spirit. Because **"all of the paths of the Lord are lovingkindness and truth" (Psalm 25:10),** we will ascend in life as we grow in lovingkindness and truth. Let us look today for the opportunities that we have to show these and to grow in each. We are the ones who will benefit, who will soar higher, and find even more freedom.

DAY 16

A Special Grace

Therefore, let everyone who is godly pray to Thee in a time when Thou mayest be found; surely in a flood of great waters they shall not reach him (Psalm 32:6).

There is often a tendency in Christians not to really seek the Lord until we get into a crisis situation. Then we seek Him earnestly, which is a primary reason why many stay in a seemingly perpetual state of crisis. We see this same pattern with Israel in the Old Testament. As we are told in Matthew 7:21-27:

"Not everyone who says to Me, 'Lord, Lord,' will enter the kingdom of heaven; but he who does the will of My Father who is in heaven.

"Many will say to Me on that day, 'Lord, Lord,' did we not prophesy in Your name, and in Your name cast out demons, and in Your name perform many miracles?'

"And then I will declare to them, 'I never knew you; depart from Me, you who practice lawlessness.'

"Therefore everyone who hears these words of Mine, and acts upon them, may be compared to a wise man, who built his house upon the rock.

"And the rain descended, and the floods came, and the winds blew, and burst against that house; and yet it did not fall, for it had been founded upon the rock.

"And everyone who hears these words of Mine, and does not act upon them, will be like a foolish man, who built his house upon the sand.

"And the rain descended, and the floods came, and the winds blew, and burst against that house; and it fell, and great was its fall."

As we read here, just calling Jesus Lord does not guarantee that we will enter the kingdom of heaven. We must do His will. To call Him Lord and not do what He says disqualifies us from being a believer, which makes us an obvious unbeliever. How could we really know the glorious King of kings and not do what He says? To know that He is God and not obey Him would be an ultimate delusion. This delusion leads to many tragedies and failures when the floods of life come.

One of our ultimate quests should therefore be to hear the words of the Lord. As we are told in John 10:4: **"When he** (the good Shepherd) **puts forth all his own, he goes before them, and the sheep follow him because they know his voice."** The obvious counterpoint here is that if we do not know His voice, we will not follow Him. However, hearing His words and obeying them are two different things. Many glory in how well they hear the Lord, but they do not do what He says. We must count His words as the unfathomable treasures that they are. When the Lord gives us direction, we should write it in a journal, reviewing it often to see how we have complied with our King's directives.

If you are in confusion about how to hear from the Lord, go back and review the things that you know He has directed you to do. These are things like prayer, reading the Bible, fellowship, etc., all of which are directives that are clearly given to us in Scripture. As we obey these we will begin walking in the light, and the light will make our paths, and His voice increasingly clear. As we are told in Proverbs 4:18:

But the path of the righteous is like the light of dawn, that shines brighter and brighter until the full day.

If we are on the right road, things should be getting brighter. If we are on the wrong road, things will be getting darker and more confused. If our path is not getting brighter and clearer every day, then we have departed from the right path somewhere. In the Lord the wrong path never turns into the right path. The only way for us to get back on the right path is to go back to the point where we made the wrong turn. That is called repentance.

Repentance is not only a good thing; it is one of the greatest Christian truths. In Christ we can actually go back to where we made a mistake and start over and get it right. In Acts 11:18, we read the response of the Jewish believers after hearing Peter's testimony about going to the house of Cornelius: **"And when they heard this, they quieted down, and glorified God, saying, 'Well then, God has granted to the Gentiles also the repentance that leads to life.'"** Eight of the most powerful Words in Scripture are found in this verse: **"God has granted...the repentance that leads to life."** Repentance is a special grace that God grants and it leads to life.

DAY 17

Fear and Love

In John 7:17, the Lord gives us a most basic principle for understanding truth, **"If any man is willing to do His will, he shall know of the teaching, whether it is of God, or whether I speak from Myself."** If we are going to know the truth, we must be committed to living that truth. It is not those who just know the truth about the cross who are saved, but those who have had the truth of the cross applied to their lives. When this truth is applied to our lives, we are born again into a life of union and obedience to God. As we are told in Psalm 25:12-13:

> **Who is the man who fears the LORD? He will instruct him in the way he should choose.**
> **His soul will abide in prosperity, and his descendants will inherit the land.**

The fear of the Lord is required if we are to receive His guidance and instruction or receive our inheritance. The goal of truth is not just so we can know the way, but also so that we will walk in the way. Without a solid foundation of the pure and holy fear of the Lord, we will build our lives on the weak foundation of knowing the truth but not doing it. Therefore, the true nature of our spiritual lives is revealed in the way we behave when no one is looking and when we know no one could find out. Who we are in secret before God is who we are.

As the next verse states, the one who fears the Lord and receives His instruction will abide in prosperity, and his children will inherit the land. This is the foundation of the true nobility. The original purpose of the nobility was to plant righteous families in the earth who would be righteous generation after generation. These were also the land owners because the righteous were to inherit the land. Of course, this was perverted whenever a generation did not walk in the fear of the Lord. However, to plant a family in the earth that walks in the fear of the Lord is still our calling and should be the goal of every Christian. As we walk in the fear of the Lord and pass this on to our children, our families will prosper, inherit the land, and be a righteous seed in the earth.

As we are told in Proverbs 22:1, **"A good name is to be more desired than great riches, favor is better than silver and gold."** Those who fear the Lord determine that they will establish a name that is esteemed for truth, honor, integrity, and true Christian charity. We must impart to our children the knowledge that the true fear of the Lord is our most valuable possession, and to live our lives to serve and obey Him is the highest calling. Those who walk in this are the true nobility. Their names are not just known on the earth, they are written in the Book of Life.

The first Adam had a bride that lived in a perfect world, yet chose to sin. The **"last Adam," (I Corinthians 15:45)** Jesus, will have a bride who lived in a most imperfect world, but chose to obey. This is our calling and is a success whose treasure will last forever.

DAY 18

Friends of God

Surely the Lord GOD does nothing unless He reveals His secret counsel to His servants the prophets (Amos 3:7).

This Scripture is amazing. Why would the Creator of the universe obligate Himself not to do anything without first revealing it to the prophets? The reason for this is understood in His purpose for creating man. He created man for fellowship. He created man to walk and talk with Him, and to have the ability to both understand and appreciate the Lord and His purposes.

The prophets have been one of the primary ways that the Lord has continued to call man back to this fellowship. Therefore, the Lord declares that He will disclose His purposes to the prophets, who are to convey them so that man can return to the place of fellowship and appreciation of his Maker.

For this reason we should understand that what the Lord is saying through prophecy is always important, but most importantly is the fact that He is still speaking to us. The quality of any relationship is determined by the quality of the communication. For this reason the Lord said in John 10:4, **"When he puts forth all his own, he goes before them, and the sheep follow him because they know his voice."** We will follow Him to the degree that we know His voice.

The first man who prophesied in Scripture was Enoch (see Jude 1:14). Enoch was a remarkable man about which very little is said, except that he walked with God and the Lord took him so that he should not see death. Enoch was from the seventh generation after Adam, but since Adam lived more than nine hundred years, Adam was still alive during Enoch's life. It is likely that Enoch talked with Adam and was stirred by the relationship that Adam had with the Lord before the Fall. Something in Enoch must have determined that he was going to try to recover that relationship, and he did.

Enoch became so close to God that the Lord just took him so he would not have to taste death—the sure consequence of the Fall. This infers that by walking with God, Enoch rose above the sin nature and escaped the consequences of it. He must have been shown the salvation through Jesus and His cross because there is no other way for man to overcome the power of death except through the cross. How did this happen?

Those who walk with God will prophesy, just as Enoch did. As we are told in Revelation 19:10, **"For the testimony of Jesus is the spirit of prophecy."** For Enoch to have prophesied, he must have had the testimony of Jesus. All of the prophets had to have the testimony of Jesus and that is why they all prophesied of His coming. They saw Him and believed in Him, looking ahead to the cross just as we look back at it.

Though Enoch was the first man that is said to have prophesied, the first man called a prophet in Scripture is Abraham (see Genesis 20:7). This is also the very first verse in which prayer is mentioned in Scripture. It is no accident that the first mention of both prophet and prayer are together. Prayer is communication. The development of communication with God, both to Him and from Him, is the foundation upon which all true prophetic ministry is based.

Abraham was also the first to be called the **"friend of God" (James 2:23).** This is the essence of true prophetic ministry. The reason the Lord said that He would not do anything unless He first revealed it to His servants the prophets is because the prophets are His friends, and He does not want to do anything without sharing it with His friends. This fellowship is the essence of why He created man. This is why Paul the apostle said: **"you may all prophesy" (I Corinthians 14:31).** Because of the cross, the veil has been rent. We can now all enter into the most intimate fellowship with Him. We can all walk with God and be such a friend of His that He does not want to do anything without sharing it with us. That is the essence of the true prophetic ministry—simple friendship with God.

DAY 19

Intimacy Versus Familiarity

Yesterday we discussed Amos 3:7 where the Lord said that He would not do anything without first revealing His **"secret counsel"** to His servants the prophets. We also see in Psalm 25:14 that **"the secret of the LORD is for those who fear Him, and He will make them know His covenant."** Those who fear Him are the ones He can trust with divine knowledge.

We may wonder how we can really be friends with Him if we fear Him, but it is the understanding of these divine paradoxes on which the path of life is found. The Hebrew word that is translated **"fear"** in Psalm 25:14 is *yare'* (yaw-ray'). Some translations have rendered this word "respect," which of course it is, but it is respect to the tenth power. Even if we are His best friends, He is still God and we are still men.

John was the intimate friend of Jesus. Judas was familiar. There is an unholy familiarity with God that can be the foundation of the most tragic falls from grace. On the other hand, when John was old and the only original apostle left, he was caught up into the vision that is recorded as the book of Revelation. He would still repeatedly fall prostrate in the Presence of the Lord. The one who was arguably the man with the greatest revelation of Christ and the most intimate friend of God, never lost his fear of the Lord. This is probably the main reason why he was trusted with such revelations.

In one of Paul's first epistles, he claims that he is not inferior to even the most eminent apostles. Later he writes that he is **"the least of the apostles" (I Corinthians 15:9).** Then a few years later he writes that he is **"the very least of all saints" (Ephesians 3:8).** In one of his last letters he writes that he is **"the worst of sinners" (I Timothy 1:16 NIV).** Do you see a progression in this? The greater the spiritual maturity, the greater the humility.

What king or President would allow someone who was not discreet to get near their throne or anywhere close to where sensitive discussions were taking place? If we want to be that friend the Lord shares His **"secret counsel"** with, we must understand both the honor and responsibility that it is. If we are going to be trusted with prophetic revelation, we need to have as much wisdom to know when not to share something as when to share. This wisdom is rooted in the fear of the Lord. We can be His best friend, but we must never forget who He is. The fear of the Lord is the beginning of wisdom, and it is the foundation of all true prophetic ministry.

DAY 20

Peace on Earth

My eyes are continually toward the LORD, for He will pluck my feet out of the net (Psalm 25:15).

There is no trap the enemy can lay for us that the Lord cannot deliver us from. However, deliverance requires that we look to Him and not man or our own devices.

One cannot live in this world without having difficulties. When the Son of God Himself walked the earth, He suffered continual attacks from His enemies. They were constantly trying to trap Him, discredit Him, and even kill Him. We can look at His life and think that He never had any peace, but in fact He was never without peace. He was the Prince of Peace, and peace could not be taken from Him by trials. Neither can the peace that He has given to us be taken by trials, unless we surrender it.

As I am writing this I am watching a bluebird seeking out its breakfast in the grass. What a wonderful existence this bird seems to have, flying around happily enjoying all that God created. However, reality is that every time the bird lands, it has to watch out for a host of creatures that would like to make it their breakfast. Even when it flies, hawks and falcons must constantly be watched.

What's my point? Presently, the whole earth is in conflict. As humans we may complain about our "dog eat dog" existence of competition, but the rest of the creatures have to worry about being literally eaten every day. Even so, as Christians we have the greatest promise of all, the promise of a world to come that is greater than any utopia or civilization that even the most optimistic philosophers have been able to envision. A kingdom is coming that will bring peace to the earth. It will bring such peace that the lion will lie down with the lamb, and children will be able to play with cobras. No one will hurt anyone else again on the earth.

It is the goal of the Christian life to live in the age to come now. It is our job to live in it to the degree that we can preach it with conviction and demonstrate it with power. We are ambassadors of this kingdom that is going to come to earth. Every day we must arise and keep our attention on living in the realm where peace is already available that is beyond comprehension to those who merely live on this earth.

We are called to live every day walking closely with the Prince of Peace Himself. Because He is the Prince of Peace, He brings peace wherever He goes. Therefore, if we take Him to work with us we will bring peace to the workplace. When conflict arises, we will not get caught up in it, but rather be peacemakers. Our job now is to help the lions and lambs start lying down together in peace.

It is noteworthy that the apostle said, **"And the God of peace will soon crush Satan under your feet" (Romans 16:20).** It seems that it would be **"the Lord of hosts,"** which means "Lord of armies," that would crush Satan, but rather it is **"the God of peace."** The peace of God is an impregnable fortress and irresistible force. The power of God's peace is greater than all of the conflict on this earth.

Do not let anything steal the peace of God that has been given to you. We have this peace by keeping our attention on the One who is above all rule and authority and power. It is our calling to live in His peaceful domain, and to carry it forth into this present darkness. Those who live by His peace have the sure promise from the Lord that a better day is coming to this earth. That is the kingdom He preached, and we too must proclaim by the demonstration of our lives that our peace cannot be shaken by the conflicts of this present age. For this reason the apostles continually gave the salutation, "May the peace of God be with you."

DAY 21

Purified Wine

There is a remarkable warning in Jeremiah 48:11-12:

Moab hath been at ease from his youth, and he hath settled on his lees, and hath not been emptied from vessel to vessel, neither hath he gone into captivity: therefore his taste remained in him, and his scent is not changed.

Therefore, behold, the days come, saith the LORD, that I will send unto him wanderers, that shall cause him to wander, and shall empty his vessels, and break their bottles (KJV).

The way that wine was purified in ancient times was to let it sit in a vessel until the impurities settled to the bottom, and then it was poured into a new vessel. Next it would be allowed to sit again until the remaining impurities had settled, and then it would get poured into another vessel. Therefore, each time it had been poured into a new vessel it would be more pure. This is also a way that the Lord uses to work the impurities out of our lives—He takes us through changes.

Sociologists have long been baffled at the extraordinary resistance many people have toward change. They are still hard pressed to explain why the child of alcoholic parents will so often marry a heavy drinker, knowing all of the pain and turmoil that can be expected. However, the fear of change, which is popularly referred to as "the tyranny of the familiar," is often stronger than the fear of such pain and turmoil. It is precisely what turns Christians into "old wineskins." New wine is still expanding, and an old wineskin is one that is too rigid and inflexible to hold new wine.

It is comforting to know that the Lord never changes. However, if we are going to be like Him, most of us still have a lot of changing to do! Until we are like Him and doing the works that He did, we are not through with the process yet. Therefore, we can expect a lifetime of changing. One of the ways that the Lord keeps us flexible is to "pour us into a new vessel" whenever we start becoming too comfortable and resistant to change. We may think that the shocking changes that come into our lives are the result of the devil's attack, but even if they were, the Lord had to allow them, so we can assume that we needed them. Many of these changes are possibly even the answer to our prayers by not allowing us to become old wineskins.

If we would remain open to the changes He wants to bring into our lives without resisting them, including the new things He is doing that we may not understand yet, we probably would not have to endure nearly the amount of shaking that we end up having to go through. If we are wise we will learn to embrace change as the great opportunity for spiritual growth that it is. Usually when we are resistant to change, it is because we are placing our security in our environment instead of in the Lord.

The Moabites were so resistant to change that the Lord had to tip over their vessels and shatter their jars. This resistance is still a reason for many church splits and even the disbanding of churches. It is easy to discern that the unity in many churches is based more in nostalgia than the Presence or the purpose of the Lord. When we get too comfortable and complacent with one group of friends, the Lord often has to shake us up or pour us into a new vessel. This may have been a reason why the Lord had to scatter the first century Jerusalem church. The Lord is deeply concerned about the unity of His church. However, the kind of exclusive unity that many congregations fall into often causes them to neglect the unity that we must have with the rest of the body of Christ. When this happens, the Lord will often have no choice but to allow someone or something to tip the jars over.

I do not think that I know a single Christian who has not been through some kind of traumatic church problem or split. Even so, the wise do not base their vision or theology on the mistakes of the past, but learn the necessary lessons, allowing the experience to purify them so that they have a more clear vision for the future. We must continue to move forward. Every time the wine is poured into a new vessel there is a great deal of commotion, but the purity is worth it. If we respond right, the time will come when we do not put our security in our environment as much as in the Lord, and we are so flexible and teachable that He will not have to tip over our vessels or shatter our jars.

DAY 22

Wearing Out the Saints

My people hath been lost sheep: their shepherds have caused them to go astray, they have turned them away on the mountains: they have gone from mountain to hill, they have forgotten their resting place (Jeremiah 50:6 KJV).

This warning from Jeremiah is just as valid today as it was when he gave it. One of the primary ways that God's people are led astray is in this same way: They are taken **"from mountain to hill,"** or one high experience to another, and not to their true resting place—union with the Lord of the Sabbath Himself.

It is easy to mobilize people around projects, especially spiritual projects and outreaches. Modern advertising has conditioned most people to respond to hype and self-promotion. Unfortunately, many ministries have learned to use these techniques very well to draw people to their projects. They work. However, when the dust clears the people are left even emptier than before. One of the primary reasons for the spiritual lukewarmness that so many Christians are now trapped in is because they are simply worn out going from one project to the next.

The greatest responsibility on earth is to lead, direct, and care for God's own people. The pastoral ministry is deserving of far more respect, honor, and support than we could ever give it. Presently, it is possibly the most difficult, yet thankless job on earth. However, the modern form that this ministry has taken is so seriously flawed that it is not only leading many of the Lord's sheep astray, it is destroying the shepherds as well.

Recently, Bob Jones, a prophetic friend, was visited by one of the largest angels that he had ever seen. This angel said that his name was "The Winds of Change" and that great changes were coming to the church. He said that until now we have known mostly the winds of adversity, but the winds of change that were coming would "fill our sails" as the church is about to move forward again.

Bob was also given a vision of a bridge collapsing in North Carolina. A few days later it happened. As people were walking over a bridge to the Charlotte Motor Speedway it collapsed, injuring more than one hundred people. When the Lord shows us something like this, it is not just to impress us prophetically—it is because there is a message in it.

In dreams and visions, cars often represent ministries, which are vehicles for carrying people. NASCAR is now the number one spectator sport in America. I, too, love racing, but if you think about it, it is nothing more than watching cars exert a lot of energy going nowhere fast. Is that not the state that many modern ministries are in today? They are putting out a lot of power, and are moving really fast, but in circles! What is really being accomplished by them? For many it has become nothing but a mad attempt to find the next thing that will keep the people hyped and moving. Why are so many people drawn to this type of spectacle, or this type of ministry?

I would love to drive a racecar. When I went to a NASCAR race I was very surprised by how exciting it was to just watch. I am also amazed at how genuinely entertaining some ministries are. You can become mesmerized watching them, but what are they really saying? Where are they leading us? If we build our churches or ministries on entertainment, it is on the shakiest of foundations. If you build this way, it will only take a few meetings that are less than "mountain top" experiences before you will not have many people left. The greatest enemy of these churches is not sin or the devil, but boredom.

I have watched many ministries go faster and faster in their little circle. Like racecars, they bump and push other ministries out of the way in their drive to stay in front. Modern ministry is actually a bigger spectator sport than NASCAR. Week after week, millions fill the pews to watch a few run around up front. It may be entertaining, but is this what New Testament church life was intended to be? No, and the winds of change are coming.

If you are a pastor or leader trapped in this mad cycle of ministry that must go ever faster, while it is really just going in circles, you are going to need more than a pit stop. You can make a few stops for more fuel and tires, but there is a point when your engine will not be able to take it any more. One insurance executive told me that they are now starting to rate pastors as high risk, claiming that a thirty-year-old pastor can have a sixty-year-old heart. You must get off of this racetrack and get on to the highway. You must stop pursuing ministry and start pursuing the Lord. It may sound too simple, but it is the only way out. As the apostle wrote:

> **For I am jealous for you with a godly jealousy; for I betrothed you to one husband, that to Christ I might present you as a pure virgin.**
>
> **But I am afraid, lest as the serpent deceived Eve by his craftiness, your minds should be led astray from the simplicity and purity of devotion to Christ (II Corinthians 11:2-3).**

As we discussed earlier, craftiness is using human wisdom to bend the rules to try and get an edge. The first thing that was said about the serpent in the garden was that he was more crafty than the other beasts. Many modern ministries have been built on this, but like the serpent, it only leads to the curse of eating dust. It is time to return to the Tree of Life, the Lord Jesus Himself.

DAY 23

God's Heart

> "And the glory which Thou hast given Me I have given to them; that they may be one, just as We are one;
> I in them, and Thou in Me, that they may be *perfected in unity*, that they world may know that Thou didst send Me, and didst love them, even as Thou didst love Me" (John 17:22-23).

These two verses are worth a lifetime of study and contemplation. This was a focus of the prayer the Lord made the night before He was crucified. If we knew that we had less than twenty-four hours to live, our prayers would probably be the most focused that they have ever been on the deepest issues of our hearts. We can therefore consider the Lord's prayer that night to be just that—the revelation of the deepest concerns of His heart. Therefore, John 17 may be the most pure reflection of the heart of God. Obviously one of the deepest issues of His heart was for the unity of His people. He has even given us His glory for this purpose—so that we will be one.

As Paul wrote in II Corinthians 3:18, it is the glory of the Lord that changes us:

> But we all, with unveiled face beholding as in a mirror the glory of the Lord, are being transformed into the same image from glory to glory, just as from the Lord, the Spirit.

One of the basic characteristics of God is unity. The Father, Son, and Holy Spirit are always in perfect unity. There is never any jealousy, contention, strife, or discord in the Trinity. The closer we become to being changed into the image of the Lord, the more unity we will have with Him and one another. By beholding His glory, this will be accomplished. He gave us His glory that we might be one, and to the degree that we have beheld His glory we will have unity.

The reverse is also true. If there is discord in the church, it is because we have taken our eyes off of the Lord and are no longer beholding His glory. Knowing that one of the deepest desires of the

Lord's heart is the unity of His people, how could anyone who truly loves the Savior willfully bring discord to the church that He died to save and unify? Ephesians 4:29-32 punctuates this crucial truth:

> **Let no unwholesome word proceed from your mouth, but only such a word as is good for edification according to the need of the moment, that it may give grace to those who hear.**
>
> **And do not grieve the Holy Spirit of God, by whom you were sealed for the day of redemption.**
>
> **Let all bitterness and wrath and anger and clamor and slander be put away from you, along with all malice.**
>
> **And be kind to one another, tender-hearted, forgiving each other, just as God in Christ also has forgiven you.**

Bitterness, wrath, anger, clamor, and slander grieve the Holy Spirit because it destroys the unity of His people. Therefore, we should always endeavor to obey the exhortation here by not letting any unwholesome word proceed from our mouths, but only those that bring edification to His people.

As a parent there are few things that bless me more than seeing my children loving and getting along with each other. Likewise, there are few things that bring me more grief than when they begin to fight or get angry with each other. Remember, the unity of His people is one of the deepest issues of God's heart. If we love Him, should we not utterly devote ourselves to that which is so obviously important to Him?

DAY 24

Having the Mind of Christ

But we have the mind of Christ (I Corinthians 2:16).

Note here that the apostle said **"we have the mind of Christ,"** not "I." No one person can have the whole mind of Christ, but each of us has been given a part. Therefore, we must come together in unity to have His complete mind. To the degree that we are connected in fellowship with the rest of His church is to the degree that we will have His whole council. Unity is not an ideal, it is essential if we are to have the whole truth or walk in the whole council of God. This is why Jesus prayed for His people to be **"perfected in unity" (John 17:23).**

Several years ago it became popular to recognize and try to get free of what has been called "co-dependence." This is an unhealthy attachment to another person, or group, in which our own personality is swallowed up in the identity of another. This can be done with a spouse, friend, boss, parent, child, or groups such as clubs, associations, etc. We can also have an unhealthy, co-dependent relationship with the church. Cults are usually composed of co-dependent people who are seeking their own identity through the group. Domineering leaders, who are decisive and seem to know where they are going, attract weak, co-dependent people.

The point has been rightly made that to get free from our tendency toward co-dependency, we must go through a period of independence to really find out who we are. This is true, but we must not stop there. The highest attainment is not independence, but inter-dependence. In fact, we cannot fully know our own identity until we are *properly* related to other people.

Co-dependency is not true unity; it is dominance of the weak by the strong. We each need to have a period in our life when we seek our own gifts and callings and become secure in who we are and what we have been called to do. Only then is true unity possible. Unity is not the melding together of people so that personal identity is lost; it is the recognition and working together of the different and unique parts of the body so that it functions as a unit.

For my body to function properly, my heart cannot ever try to become a lung. My heart needs the lungs, kidneys, liver, and blood vessels to function correctly, but it must not ever try to be anything but a heart. I can have five of the healthiest hearts in the world, but if they are not attached to at least one good lung, then those hearts are going to die. The Lord has composed His body, the church, in the same way. It is supposed to be many different, unique parts that know their identities, but also know their place in the whole.

I have asked a number of large groups of Christians in churches and conferences how many knew their calling or ministry in the body of Christ. Most of the time the response was less than 5 percent. The highest it has ever been was about 20 percent. How well could you live if only 5 percent of your body was functioning, or even 20 percent? This is the state of the body of Christ. We are in need of unity, but we must first go through the stage where each member of the body comes to know their place and purpose in the body.

I have contended for years that there is a need for different denominations and movements within the church. Because the members of the body have not graduated from the "independence" stage of maturity in which identity is fundamentally established, we need to stay there until it is. However, we have been there for centuries now. It is time to get the job completed and press on toward the ultimate fulfillment that can only be found in inter-dependence with the rest of the church.

A heart "knows" that it is a heart and not a lung because it recognizes the place of the lung and works together with it. Even though we need to go through the independent stage, we will not fully know who we are and our place until we are firmly established in inter-dependence. All true New Testament ministry is a team of different parts that function together as a unit. Barnabas had to go and find Saul (who later became Paul), and then both of them had to get in the right place (Antioch), before they could be released into their own ultimate callings as apostles. In the same way, we, too, must seek out those whom we are called to be joined with in the Lord before we can be released into our ultimate purpose.

I have heard an alarming number of Christians say that they love the Lord but they just do not like the church. As John wrote, this is not possible. We do not really love the Lord if we do not love His people. The Lord Himself said that as we treat the least of His people it is counted as the way that we treat Him. We do not have to love the state that the church is in, but we must love His church. If we do not, we will never be useful in helping her attain her purpose, which can only be accomplished as we come into unity.

The Scriptures are clear that the church will attain unity before the end comes. The Lord's prayer will be answered and we will be perfected in unity. Let us all determine that we will be a part of helping this come to pass, and not a stumbling block to it.

DAY 25

The Beginning of True Church Life

Yesterday we considered I Corinthians 2:16, **"But we have the mind of Christ,"** and John 17:23 where the Lord prayed that we would be **"perfected in unity."** We then briefly discussed the three basic stages of personality development, which are: co-dependence, independence, and inter-dependence. Today I want to view this a little deeper, applying it practically to a major thrust that the church is about to go through. In Ephesians 4:11-16 we read how this is supposed to happen in the church.

> **And He gave some as apostles, and some as prophets, and some as evangelists, and some as pastors and teachers,**
>
> **for the equipping of the saints for the work of service, to the building up of the body of Christ;**
>
> **until we all attain to the unity of the faith, and of the knowledge of the Son of God, to a mature man, to the measure of the stature which belongs to the fulness of Christ.**
>
> **As a result, we are no longer to be children, tossed here and there by waves, and carried about by every wind of doctrine, by the trickery of men, by craftiness in deceitful scheming;**
>
> **but speaking the truth in love, we are to grow up in all aspects into Him, who is the head, even Christ,**
>
> **from whom the whole body, being fitted and held together by that which every joint supplies, according to the proper working of each individual part, causes the growth of the body for the building up of itself in love.**

We see that the five ministries named here are given to equip the members of the body who are called to do the actual ministry. Therefore the primary job of an evangelist is not to just evangelize, but to impart a love for the lost to the whole body, and help all believers to be able to lead others to the Lord. The main job of a prophet is not just to hear from the Lord, but also to help all believers to know the Lord's voice and be able to prophesy. The primary job of a teacher is not just to impart knowledge, but also to impart a love for the truth and the spiritual tools needed for all believers to be able to mine the truths of God's Word. The primary task of a pastor is not just to lead people, but also to equip all believers to be able to help one another. The apostle is called to do all of these.

As we read in verse 13, this is to be done **"until we all attain to the unity of the faith, and of the knowledge of the Son of God, to a mature man, to the measure of the stature which belongs to the fulness of Christ."** Note that he does not say here until "some" attain, but **"all."** We cannot get where we are supposed to go without each other. We are therefore compelled to love and help one another if even for selfish reasons. If we fully understood this we would look at the weakest Christians or churches as those we must reach out to help. We cannot write off those who may have some wrong doctrines and practices. This does not mean that we have to accept their errors, but we must accept and pray for them, seeking any way that we can be used to help them.

When there were only two brothers on the earth they could not get along, and one killed the other. Today almost all unity is based on the selfish need for one another. When that need is no longer there, division and fighting is usually inevitable. However, this need will never cease to be in the church. Selfishness is not the highest motive by any means, but it can at least help maintain enough unity until we mature in love and the higher motives. We must understand that whenever we hurt another member of the body of Christ, we are hurting ourselves as well. Whenever one member is hurt in any way, we too are hurt, and we therefore must begin to protect and defend one another in the faith.

If we have the Holy Spirit then we have the One who is called **"the Helper" (John 14:26).** If we are taking on His nature it should become our nature to help one another. Why not begin to pray for the denomination, church, or even individual Christians that we may have the most problems with? Why not ask the Lord to show us practical ways that we can begin to help them? As the Scripture affirms, what is accomplished if we only love those who are lovable to us? (see Luke 6:32) Let us try to grow in love by loving those that may not be as lovable to us, and then excel in love by loving and helping those who have even offended us. Pursuing love in this way is the path to finding our true identity in Christ.

DAY 26

Change Is Coming

Yesterday we addressed why we must have unity in the church, as well as some practical ways to help bring and preserve unity, especially as outlined in Ephesians 4:11-13. We can become great at leadership and organization, but no amount of human organization or leadership will cause the church to grow up to **"the measure of the stature which belongs to the fulness of Christ" (Ephesians 4:13).** Only the Spirit can bring forth that which is spirit (see John 3:6), and only the Lord can build His church. When He builds His church He does it through the ministries that He has given for this purpose, which are the ones listed in Ephesians 4.

Presently, most churches are led by one person who, with his or her staff, does the majority of the ministry. A few are equipping some in the church to do a few aspects of the ministry, but mostly what would be considered the ministry of helps. Churches that are devoted to building home groups usually do more for equipping their people, but this cannot be a substitute for the ministry of those who are given for the equipping of the church. Some may bring in visiting ministries occasionally, such as an evangelist to stir up evangelism in their people. This is commendable, but there is a difference between stirring up and equipping.

I know quite a few traveling ministries who either claim to be, or aspire to be, one of the equipping ministries listed in Ephesians 4. However, with the exception of just a few, their program consists mostly of going to a church and having a good meeting, or maybe even a series of meetings where their gifts are demonstrated. This can be helpful and people are encouraged by it, but not equipped. For the church to mature in the way to which we are called, there must be a radical transformation of our concept of ministry. This is something that much of the church worldwide is now grappling with and addressing, and it is something we must do.

We should question whether one is really an Ephesians 4 equipping ministry unless they are leaving behind those who can do what they do. This takes time, and it takes a depth of relationship that is not possible if one just passes through for a couple of days once or twice a year. That is why in the book of Acts we see the traveling ministries sometimes parking in one place for months or even years.

If we are not in a church that has the vision for equipping their people in all of the aspects we see in Ephesians 4, we can still receive from equipping ministries through other means. We are blessed today to have books, tapes, conferences, television, etc., all readily available. These can all be helpful, but for the church to **"attain to the measure of the stature which belongs to the fulness of Christ,"** it is obvious that there is a radical change needed in the general concept of ministry that most of the church now has.

Remember, change is good and change is coming.

DAY 27

The Maturing of the Saints

"But woe to those who are with child and to those who nurse babes in those days!" (Matthew 24:19)

This was a warning that the Lord Jesus gave when He was describing the last days. Another way I think we could phrase this is "Woe to those pastors who keep their people in immaturity!"

Yesterday, we addressed the need for the equipping ministries listed in Ephesians 4 if the church is to function and mature as it is supposed to do. I want to now elaborate a little on the next verse in this chapter, Ephesians 4:14:

> **As a result, we are no longer to be children, tossed here and there by waves, and carried about by every wind of doctrine, by the trickery of men, by craftiness in deceitful scheming.**

This verse is a good depiction of much of the body of Christ today. It is accurate to say that most Christians remain spiritual children. They get tossed about by waves and movements, but seldom mature, and few ever walk in their calling. Those who are not tossed about by waves and movements are tossed about by winds of doctrine that carry them from one emphasis to another. These are the ones who are doing relatively well! The rest are captured by the **"trickery of men, by craftiness in deceitful scheming."**

As we read in the previous verses, one of the reasons the equipping ministries are given to the church is so that this will not happen. It will continue to happen, however, until these ministries are restored and given their rightful place of authority and influence in the church.

We begin to feel good about ourselves if we think that we know some apostles, prophets, or evangelists, etc., and that our church recognizes and receives from them. This may be true of some, but if we are to examine the fruit of those who call themselves apostles, prophets, evangelists, pastors, or teachers, do we see what is described

73

here in Ephesians 4? Is there any church on earth where all of the members are really being equipped for the ministry as it states in this chapter? Is there a congregation anywhere that is really growing up into the **"measure of the stature that belongs to the fullness of Christ?" (Ephesians 4:12)**

I am including the congregations that I have been a part of planting in this assessment as well. We have done fairly well in equipping some of the people to do some things, but overall we, too, fall far short of this level of ministry that is supposed to be the standard for all churches. Therefore, I am not writing this to condemn anyone's church or ministry, but rather as a cry that we must wake up. We only have a couple of the equipping ministries functioning in our church at this time. We have invited those who would like to visit and help us in what we are lacking, and they do, but not in the kind of depth that it really takes to equip the people to do the work of the ministry.

As I stated yesterday, I only know of a handful of ministries throughout the world who really seem to understand and are committed to equipping believers to do the work of the ministry. Most just think that it is their job to perform their ministry, and if people catch on to what they are doing and are able to then do some of it, great. It is apparent that less than 10 percent of the Christians in the church today even know what their calling is, and less than this are actually functioning in their calling. This is a spiritual tragedy.

I watched my father endure a number of strokes until he could only move one arm a little. To see him in this condition for several months was one of the hardest things I can ever remember going through. How does the Lord feel when He looks down on the church that is supposed to be His glorious bride and she can barely move an arm a little? If we have been trusted with an equipping ministry in the church, are we not responsible for this?

The present form of ministry in the church, as it is understood and functioning, is not accomplishing its biblical mandate. There must be a radical change in our understanding of ministry. As the saying goes, "Unless you change your course you will end up where you are headed." We are in need of a drastic course correction in the very way that church leadership and ministry are now conducted.

Our condition is not just the result of the church failing to understand and accept apostolic and prophetic ministries today. It is deeper than that. We do not really understand evangelists, pastors, or teachers either. It appears that those who have these callings seldom even understand their own purpose in more than just a superficial way.

Jesus is the model of all true New Testament ministry. When you think of Him, you must also think of His *disciples*. Immediately after He began His ministry He started calling disciples whom He could train to do everything that He did. This should be fundamental to all who are in ministry. Whenever we are sent out to do ministry, we should have around us those who are not just called to be assistants, but who are there to learn to do everything that we are doing so they can go out and do the same.

There are not many who are secure enough in their ministry to do this. I have questioned quite a few who feel that if they do this then those who they disciple will end up taking many of "their people." One who is this insecure should not be in ministry in the first place. If the Lord really commissioned our ministry, then He will take care of us. If we do not have this fundamental security in our lives, then we need to question whether the Lord has really sent us, or if we have just assumed a position by our own efforts.

One of the great models of New Testament ministry was actually the last prophet under the Old Covenant, as well as the first under the New Covenant, John the Baptist. His whole purpose was to prepare for the One who was to come after him, to point to Him, and then be willing to decrease as He increased. Contrary to this, church history testifies that almost every movement persecutes the succeeding movements instead of helping to prepare the way for them, blessing and commissioning them. Therefore, almost every new movement that arises to help the church advance also comes with all of the problems of not only being an orphan, but one who had to live in fear of his parents trying to kill him! This must change.

Like the Lord Himself, we must understand that our fruit will not remain unless we help prepare those who are to carry our ministry further and even do **"greater works" (John 14:12).** Until we do this, the church is going to continue to be tossed about and subjected to the trickery of men instead of advancing toward her destiny. The encouragement is that there is now a great movement across the earth to recover our basic biblical mandate for ministry. It is time, and it will soon be accomplished.

DAY 28

Choosing Life or Death

Today we will continue our study of Ephesians 4 by looking at verse 15, **"but speaking the truth in love, we are to grow up in all aspects into Him, who is the head, even Christ."** As this verse implies, one of the primary ways that we grow up into Christ is by **"speaking the truth in love."** Jesus is the Truth, and if we are going to abide in Him we must be committed to truth. God is also love, so if we are going to be like Him we must do all that we do in love.

Recent polls and studies have indicated that there is no longer a distinguishable difference between the basic moral principles of Christians and non-Christians. The divorce rate among evangelical Christians has now exceeded that of non-Christians. Studies now show that Christians are just as prone to lie as non-Christians. The most sobering fact highlighted by these studies was that the majority of Christians did not think that this was wrong! Can we not accurately say that the salt is losing its savor? What does the Lord say that He will do when this happens? He will throw that salt away!

One of the basic characteristics of God is that His Word is true! How can we ever expect to abide in Him, be like Him, or represent Him, if we are not devoted to truth? The devil is the father of lies, and when we have given ourselves to lying in any form or to any degree, we are opening ourselves up to the devil, to be used by him, and to be changed into his image instead of Christ's.

In II Corinthians 5:14 Paul wrote, **"For the love of Christ controls us."** How different would we be if we were truly controlled by the love of Christ in everything that we did and said? How different would the church be if every Christian was controlled by the love of Christ, doing everything that they did out of a love for Him and the love that He is? The change would obviously be radical, and our goal must be nothing less than this. Before the end comes there is going to be a church that is without spot or blemish. She will be pure in all of her motives and actions. Why can't this be us?

It should be a basic goal of every Christian to walk in truth and love in everything that we do and say. If we are not, we will remain the hypocrites that the world thinks we are. We should also keep in mind that the Lord Himself reserved His most scathing denunciations for the religious hypocrites.

We should examine every conflict that we are now involved in to be sure that we are walking in both truth and love. Is our position truly accurate, or have we let partial truths, or even lies get in? Once our argument or position in a conflict passes the truth test, we should then determine that it also passes the love test. Then we should endeavor to test all of our words and actions this way.

This means that sometimes we will not say things that may be true unless we can also say them in love. Truth can hurt, and even kill, if it is not spoken in the right spirit. That is why **"Satan disguises himself as an angel of light" (II Corinthians 11:14).** This could also be translated, "messenger of truth." Many of the devil's most devastating attacks will have some basis in truth. Often it will have a twisted interpretation or be used to gain entry for his subsequent lies, but sometimes it is just plain truth that is incomplete or spoken in bad timing so that its effect is to cause division, discord, etc. That is why we must also determine if we are speaking the truth **"in love."** Satan can use truth as a weapon for evil, but he has a very hard time masquerading love.

Proverbs 18:21 states that, **"Death and life are in the power of the tongue, and those who love it will eat its fruit."** Our words have the power to impart death or life. When we speak, are we imparting life, hope, faith, peace, patience, etc., or are we being used to stir up strife, doubt, fear, or division? As we studied previously in Ephesians 4:29-32:

> **Let no unwholesome word proceed from your mouth, but only such a word as is good for edification according to the need of the moment, that it may give grace to those who hear.**
>
> **And do not grieve the Holy Spirit of God, by whom you were sealed for the day of redemption.**
>
> **Let all bitterness and wrath and anger and clamor and slander be put away from you, along with all malice.**
>
> **And be kind to one another, tender-hearted, forgiving each other, just as God in Christ also has forgiven you.**

DAY 29

Resurrection Life

Have you ever considered that one reason many have a hard time believing in the resurrection is because they look at the weakness of the Lord's own body, the church, with less than 10 percent of its members functioning? Of course the church is given as the most frequent reason why people do not believe the gospel, and this is understandable. However, before the end comes the church is going to be the glorious bride that she is called to be, with a body that functions with a beauty, grace, and power that will cause the world to marvel. Why not now? Today let's continue our study in Ephesians 4.

> **...We are to grow up in all aspects into Him, who is the head, even Christ,**
>
> **from whom the whole body, being fitted and held together by that which every joint supplies, according to the proper working of each individual part, causes the growth of the body for the building up of itself in love (Ephesians 4:15-16).**

To know the next step, we need to know where we are. It is quite obvious that the church today is in a state somewhere between atrophy and death. Many churches only continue to exist because they are on artificial life support, the devices of human mechanisms and programs. Even so, the most revolutionary force to advance the cause of Christianity in history will come when the equipping ministries start equipping the people instead of trying to do everything themselves.

As I recently heard a very gifted Bible teacher say, "Most churches today are one gift churches. Most of the time this one gift is a teacher." He was not stating this to highlight his own ministry, but he was stating it with great remorse. However, it is true. Few who actually call themselves pastors really are pastors. Some are evangelists, others are teachers, some may even be prophetic or apostolic, but it is rare to see someone with an authentic pastoral ministry actually shepherding a church. I, too, am a case in point.

However, nowhere does it say that the leader of a church should be a pastor. In fact, in the New Testament it does not even say what a pastor does or anything else about this ministry. It is only mentioned in the New Testament one time in Ephesians 4, where it is listed with the other equipping ministries. So, how did this one ministry that is only mentioned one time in the New Testament come to so totally dominate the ministry of the church? Maybe there are a few other things that we should question while we are at it?

Occasionally the leader of a church will have a second gift such as evangelism or maybe even a prophetic gift, and they are the ones who week after week practice and grow in their own gifts. However, the New Testament ministry that is revealed in Ephesians 4 is a team of ministries. The church is called to be a many membered body with every member "properly" functioning. The evidence that they do have a true New Testament ministry will therefore be a body of believers who are a living, functioning body.

This is no small task. We cannot expect to get from where the church is today to where we are called to be overnight. I have had this vision for a functioning body for almost thirty years. Our church in Charlotte still has less than 20 percent of the people functioning in their callings. It has been a very slow process for several reasons.

Possibly the main reason why we are still at this place is the fact that we grew from a few people to nearly two thousand very fast. If we had stayed smaller, we could have spent more time with individuals who could have sped up the process, but we are called to be a large church. However, we want to use this calling to learn how large churches can do this because we know that this is for all believers whether they are in large or small churches. Sadly, we do not know any smaller churches that are actually doing any better at this than we are.

Second, it has taken a while to change the mentality of the leadership team from just doing the ministry to actually equipping others. Now we have a core of ministries that are devoted to this, but it is still taking time to stimulate and awaken believers who are in a state of atrophy because they have never been allowed to do anything of significance before. However, when just one catches the vision they always wake up many more. When one member of the body starts to function, it releases great encouragement to the rest of the body.

In one of our services this year Robin McMillan started out by saying, "We have ten guest speakers tonight and none of them know who they are!" He then explained that he was going to choose ten people at random to share five minutes each. Everyone woke up because they knew that they could be called on. The ten who were chosen were apprehensive, but as soon as the first one started, the Lord came upon them. They were so anointed that some were drowned out by the cheers of the congregation, many of whom were standing on their chairs in excitement.

We now have about four hundred people on prophetic ministry teams. Not all of these are called as prophets, but all have demonstrated the gift of prophecy or the gift of interpretation, and they are growing in their gifts through exercise. However, even the greatest prophet only sees **"in part" (I Corinthians 13:9).** Therefore, to get the whole picture we have to put the different parts together. For prophets to function properly, they need to be rightly connected to the other equipping ministries given to the church.

If the Lord heals you, or gives you a prophetic word through someone else, it can be a great encouragement. However, it is not nearly as encouraging as when the Lord uses you to heal or give a prophetic word to someone else. There are few things that we can ever experience as encouraging as being used by God and learning that He had a special purpose for us when He called us before the foundation of the world. There will be few things that can strengthen and bond together your church as when the Lord starts using the members of the church.

Ephesians 4:15 states that the body is built up **"by that which every joint supplies."** A joint is not a part, but is where two parts come together. We cannot form a joint with another part of the body if we do not know what part we are. The arm has to be joined to the wrist, not the knee, etc. Most churches have people coming and going continually because the people are not properly joined to the body, which can only be done as a functioning part.

In every way, it is in our best interest to equip believers to do the work of the ministry and then release them with genuine authority to do what they are called to do. The Reformation is not yet complete. The church is still far from the form that it is called to be. The next great wave of the Spirit is going to be the awakening, equipping, and releasing of the whole body of Christ.

DAY 30

The Power of Fellowship

Over the last few days we have been looking at Ephesians 4:11-16 because this is one of the most concise texts in the Bible on New Testament church life. A healthy church life is crucial for a healthy Christian life. When we were called by the Lord, it was to be a member of a body of believers which includes hundreds of millions of others around the world. We have also been joined to the historic church that includes all of the believers who have served the Lord for the last two thousand years. We are not alone!

In verse 16 that we studied yesterday, we are told that the body is built up **"by that which every joint supplies."** A joint is where two parts come together. The stronger the union of these parts, the stronger the whole body will be. As we also discussed earlier, one of the primary burdens of the Lord's own heart is the unity of His people. Unity is essential for the health of the body, and it will be to the degree that we are in unity with the church that we are personally healthy, spiritually and physically. This we see in I Corinthians 11:23-30:

> **For I received from the Lord that which I also delivered to you, that the Lord Jesus in the night in which He was betrayed took bread;**
>
> **and when He had given thanks, He broke it, and said, "This is My body, which is for you; do this in remembrance of Me."**
>
> **In the same way He took the cup also, after supper, saying, "This cup is the new covenant in My blood; do this, as often as you drink it, in remembrance of Me."**
>
> **For as often as you eat this bread and drink the cup, you proclaim the Lord's death until He comes.**
>
> **Therefore whoever eats the bread or drinks the cup of the Lord in an unworthy manner, shall be guilty of the body and the blood of the Lord.**
>
> **But let a man examine himself, and so let him eat of the bread and drink of the cup.**

For he who eats and drinks, eats and drinks judgment to himself, if he does not judge the body rightly.

For this reason many among you are weak and sick, and a number sleep.

Of course the bread and cup that he is speaking about here is the ritual of communion, as we read in I Corinthians 10:16-17:

Is not the cup of blessing which we bless a sharing in the blood of Christ? Is not the bread which we break a sharing in the body of Christ?

Since there is one bread, we who are many are one body; for we all partake of the one bread.

The Greek word that is translated **"sharing"** here, and **"communion"** in other versions, is *koinonia*, which implies the closest, deepest kind of partnership or fellowship. The word "communion" was originally two words that were merged to form one, the two being "common" and "union." The word "fellowship" that this word is sometimes translated was taken from the phrase "two fellows in a ship," which implied that if they were going to get anywhere they would have to work together.

In these we also see that if we partake of the ritual of communion in an **"unworthy manner,"** we are guilty of the body and blood of the Lord and eat and drink judgment to ourselves. To do this in an **"unworthy manner"** is to **"not judge the body rightly."** We bring judgment on ourselves by trying to substitute the ritual for the reality that the ritual symbolizes. The reality is that we *have* communion or common union with the Lord and His body.

To have communion we must **"judge the body rightly."** We must discern the different parts and where we fit in. The only way that a teacher can have common union with the rest of the body is to understand that not all are called to be just like him, but that he must learn to relate properly to the prophets, pastors, evangelists, etc. Likewise, prophets must understand how much they need the teachers, pastors, etc. We must see how our ministries compliment each other instead of conflict with each other.

I know a number of great evangelists who lead many people to the Lord. However, all but a couple of these at least project a mentality that everyone who is not an evangelist like them is basically wasting their time. In the first century church when someone was converted they were **"added to the church" (Acts 2:47 KJV)**. Today it is estimated that as few as 5 percent of new "converts" actually go on to become part of the church. In the first century the evangelists worked together with all of the equipping ministries. Today very few do, and therefore we have this kind of result. Both the body and the new converts are therefore weak, sick, and a number sleep.

How much more fruitful would our evangelism be if prophets went into a place to spy it out and discern both the strongholds of darkness and the spiritual openings in an area before the evangelist came? How much more fruit would remain if after the evangelist left, pastors and teachers came to gather all of the new converts to lay a strong foundation in their lives and see that they were added to the church? Our calling is not to just bear fruit, but to bear fruit that remains.

As the text in I Corinthians implies, the main reason why Christians are weak, sick, and die prematurely, is our failure to discern the Lord's body. As the apostle wrote in I John 1:7:

> **but if we walk in the light as He Himself is in the light, we have fellowship with one another, and the blood of Jesus His Son cleanses us from all sin.**

The Greek word translated **"fellowship"** in this verse is the same *koinonia*. Fellowship is more than just meeting together, it is having a union where the different parts fit together properly and function together properly. It is in this kind of fellowship that His blood, which is His life, flows through us and cleanses us from all sin. We were forgiven of our sins at the cross, but there is a cleansing process that comes through fellowship that is essential.

For the life-giving blood to flow to my hand it must be properly connected to my arm. We, too, must become properly connected to the body. That is why we are exhorted to not "forsake the assembling of ourselves together" (see Hebrews 10:25 NKJV). This is not just talking about meetings, but about being *assembled together* just as the different parts of a car must be assembled together before it can actually be used to go somewhere. What good would all of the parts of a car do us if they were just laying together in a big pile? That is what the church is like at this time.

The church is made up of **"living stones" (I Peter 2:5),** but presently our congregations are like piles of these stones which have not yet been assembled into a temple where the Lord can manifest His

Presence. The assembling together of these living stones into a temple is going to take place. The Lord is going to again send His **"wise master builder" (I Corinthians 3:10)** which are authentic New Testament apostles. They will be much more than just great preachers, or even great leaders. They will be used to begin fitting the whole body together just as the Lord designed it to be. They will build the prophets, evangelists, pastors, and teachers into the teams they are called to be. They will train and release them to do their primary job again, which is to **"equip the saints for the work of ministry" (Ephesians 4:12 RSV).** Before the end, the church will arise to be the glorious body of Christ that it is called to be, with all of the parts working!

DAY 31

Out of Control and
Into Faith

Each morning as I pray over the different ministries in MorningStar, I am confronted by the truth that what we are doing is far beyond my ability to control. I could spend all of my time with any one of the eight major ministry divisions and it would not be enough, yet I can only give each one a tiny fraction of my time. I am also challenged by the fact that each of these ministries can have an impact on Christians around the world because of the influence that we have. As I was pondering the weight of this responsibility, I began to think of my family, and how I can only give a fraction of my time to them. The burden and guilt of this was getting heavy on me until I felt the Presence of the Lord. It was as if He was putting a hand on my shoulder, reminding me that He upholds the universe with His power, and this little ministry, and my little family, was no problem!

I have come to believe that all human responsibilities are beyond human ability. That means that there is nothing that we can do right without God. It is because I cannot micro-manage our ministry that it leaves plenty of room for Him to move. It also leaves room for others to grow in the ministry. This is not to promote irresponsibility on my part, such as not spending the right amount of time with the ministry or with my family, but the right amount is found in each of these areas by following the Lord and being obedient day by day. I will not get anything right if I do not get this part right. The Lord said in Matthew 11:29-30:

> **"Take My yoke upon you, and learn from Me, for I am gentle and humble in heart; and you shall find rest for your souls.**
> **"For My yoke is easy, and My load is light."**

When I first read how the Lord will reward His faithful servants by giving them cities to rule over in the kingdom, I was shocked. That did not sound like a reward to me, but punishment! I did not even want to oversee a neighborhood, much less a city. If I could do just what I wanted to do, it would be to spend all of my time in prayer, study, and with my family. I love the fellowship of the church, but overseeing even a small church is beyond any desire that I have, much less a large ministry with a growing number of churches. However, I have found that it is in the place of responsibility that we can have very close fellowship with the Lord. He is the King of kings, so responsibility is what He does. We are in training for reigning with Him. The reigning may not be the reward, but the fellowship with Him in reigning will be our reward. If we want to abide with Him, we must learn to find fellowship with Him in all responsibility and in all authority.

The year of 2000 was a Sabbatical year for our ministry. Although we greatly reduced our activities to honor it, I do not ever remember being busier. However, the true issue of a Sabbatical is not just resting from work, but it is learning to abide in the Lord and His rest. The Lord helped us to enter His rest by giving us so much to do that we could not possibly do it without Him.

I was reading an article on what separates people like Tiger Woods and other star athletes from their peers who sometimes have more talent. The conclusion was that it was their ability to stay focused and calm under pressure. This is also probably a key issue that separates those who bear much fruit from those who are bearing little or none. However, our focus is not just on our tasks, but also on something infinitely greater—the Lord Himself. We are not just trying to stay calm, but abide in the peace of the Lord.

Studies have shown that one minute of rage can sap the strength of a normal eight hour period. Just being angry for a few minutes can do the same thing. Worry also drains our energy at an amazing rate, even much faster than hard labor. How much more effective could we be, and how much more energy could we have, if we would abide in the peace of the Lord? Could this be why Paul wrote that **"... the God of peace will soon crush Satan under your feet" (Romans 16:20).**

This is also a reason why elders in the church cannot be **"quick-tempered" (Titus 1:7)** or given to *outbursts of anger.* There are few things that can sap our effectiveness like anger or fear. In contrast, faith releases the power that created the universe.

We often think of great faith as something that happens spontaneously so we can be used for a miracle or healing. However, the greatest and most effective faith of all is to live day by day trusting Him. It is by trusting Him so much that we look at every problem as an opportunity to see His work in our lives. It is not worrying, but rather trusting and abiding in the peace of God that will crush anything that Satan tries to do to us. If the Lord created the world out of chaos, He can easily deal with any problem that we have.

I have heard many Christians say that they know the Lord can do miracles, but they just do not know if He will. However, He has said that He always will do miracles if we believe Him. Therefore, as we read in John 6:28-29:

> **They said therefore to Him, "What shall we do, that we may work the works of God?"**
>
> **Jesus answered and said to them, "This is the work of God, that you believe in Him whom He has sent."**

Our main job is not to build a church or a ministry, but to grow in the Lord and to grow in faith. As a ministry we are just now being moved into position to begin our ultimate mission. When we look at the task, we will always be overwhelmed because it will always be much bigger than we are. It is at the point when we cannot do it that He takes over. Our goal is not the work itself, but to grow in faith in the One who alone can accomplish it.

We have been promised that we are entering a time when we will see great miracles. We need to also understand that this is probably because we are being thrust into a place where we are going to need them. Even so, this is what most of us have signed up for. We want to be a part of what God is building, not men.

Let us continue to prepare for our purpose by seeing every problem and every obstacle as an opportunity to see a miracle. Let us determine to abide in the peace of God so we can see "the God of peace crush Satan under our feet" (see Romans 16:20). We must also recognize anger and wrath as the great enemies of our purposes. We cannot allow them to gain entry into the fortress of faith that we are called to build. They are the primary enemies who will seek to drain us of our faith, focus, and even the physical energy that we have been given.

DAY 32

Anxiety Versus the Kingdom

"But seek first His kingdom and His righteousness; and all these things shall be added to you.

"Therefore do not be anxious for tomorrow; for tomorrow will care for itself. Each day has enough trouble of its own" (Matthew 6:33-34).

This passage states that if we are seeking His kingdom, we will not be anxious for tomorrow. If we are anxious, it is because we have been distracted from seeking His kingdom.

Anxiety is not a fruit of the Spirit. If we allow anxiety to lead us, the Spirit will not lead us. Anxiety is a deadly enemy, and one of the primary ways that we are led astray from our purposes. We are therefore exhorted in Philippians 4:6-7:

Be anxious for nothing, but in everything by prayer and supplication with thanksgiving let your requests be made known to God.

And the peace of God, which surpasses all comprehension, shall guard your hearts and your minds in Christ Jesus.

The peace of God is the counter to anxiety. His peace will guard our hearts and minds so that we abide in Christ Jesus. As we see in this text, His peace is the result of taking our cares to Him in prayer. How would our lives be changed if all of the time that is now consumed by worry was instead used for prayer? Most of our lives would be radically different because God answers prayer, not worry. When we pray, He changes things. He also changes us. We would see the world very differently if we saw it through the eyes of faith instead of fear.

Isaiah 6:1-3 is now some of the most important Scriptures to me, but when I was a new believer I could not understand these verses. It reads:

In the year of King Uzziah's death, I saw the Lord sitting on a throne, lofty and exalted, with the train of His robe filling the temple.

Seraphim stood above Him, each having six wings; with two he covered his face, and with two he covered his feet, and with two he flew.

And one called out to another and said, "Holy, Holy, Holy, is the LORD of hosts, the whole earth is full of His glory."

Of course, I did not have a problem believing that the Lord was holy, but with all of the wars, poverty, oppression, child abuse, sickness, and death, I could not understand how these seraphim could say that the whole earth was filled with His glory. Then one day the Lord spoke to me and said, "The reason that these seraphim see the whole earth filled with My glory is because they dwell in My Presence. If you will dwell in My Presence, you, too, will see My glory in everything."

Dwelling in the Presence of the Lord helps us to see beyond the temporary circumstances to His eternal purposes in His kingdom. This will change the way we see, the way we live and the way we are.

DAY 33

The Zone

The steadfast of mind Thou wilt keep in perfect peace, because he trusts in Thee (Isaiah 26:3).

Several years ago I was at a retreat with several dozen NFL and NBA players. Many of them were All-Stars or All-Pros. For years I have studied leadership and tried to understand what enables some to excel when others with seemingly more talent did not do as well. Just sitting around talking with some of these players led to some of the best answers I have received yet to this question.

One term that you will often hear around sports is "the zone." It is a state when mind and body seem to be in perfect harmony, and it allows a player to rise to a level of performance that is beyond his or her usual level. When a player is in "the zone," they seem unstoppable. I started questioning some of these players about "the zone," and they all used the same terms to describe it. To them it was basically a state of mind where they were able to tune out all of the usual distractions and focus completely on their task. When they could maintain this focus, they would have the feeling that no one could stop them, and usually they were right.

I then happened upon a magazine article written by a psychologist who had spent his professional life studying sports, and he, too, was especially interested in "the zone." He described it as basically "the ability to focus under pressure." The factors that he felt most affected players negatively were anger and fear. As stated previously, studies have shown how just a moment of rage can sap the same amount of strength as many hours of hard labor. Likewise, just a moment of terror or even thirty minutes of a more subtle anger or general worry, can sap us of the same amount of strength as many hours of hard labor. Therefore, for athletes to enter "the zone" they must stay completely focused on their task without giving way to either anger or fear. To the degree that they can do this is the degree they will be able to rise to greater heights of performance.

This is not just true for athletes. Anger and fear are two of the deadliest enemies of any purpose or task. How much of our energy is being sapped by anger or anxiety? How many potentially great accomplishments were derailed by unforgiveness or bitterness? How many great works of faith were derailed by fear?

Just as an athlete becomes a "superstar" when they perform their best in the biggest games, the greatest acts of faith are the result of being able to focus on the Lord in times of the greatest pressure. This is the result of learning to focus on Him more and more each day. If we do not see Him in the little things, we will not be able to see Him in the great ones.

Our goal should not only be to do everything we do for Him, but with Him. When we live by beholding the One who is above all rule and authority and dominion, when we live our lives focused on the One who is so all-powerful that He upholds the universe with the word of His power, we, too, will rise above the usual to live in the realm of miracles.

Today while you are on the job or with your family or friends, and something comes up that could anger or discourage you, look to the Lord immediately. Determine that you are not going to have your life sapped by anger or fear, but that you are going to use every opportunity to grow in faith and the peace of God. Determine that you are going to be a vessel for the Lord to use in those circumstances to impart faith and peace to others. Your life will change. Your performance will rise to previously unknown heights, not because you are staying in "the zone," but because you are abiding in the Spirit.

DAY 34

A Time for Miracles

> **And when it was evening, the disciples came to Him, saying, "The place is desolate, and the time is already past; so send the multitudes away, that they may go into the villages and buy food for themselves."**
>
> **But Jesus said to them, "They do not need to go away; you give them something to eat!" (Matthew 14:15-16)**

We are going to see some of the greatest miracles we have ever witnessed *because we are going to need them!*

Many want to see miracles, but how many are willing to be put in a place where they need one? Miracles are not given for our entertainment, neither are they given to build our faith. They are the result of our having faith. Almost every miracle was the result of a desperate need. The greater the need, the greater the miracle.

How great would the miracle have been to feed the five thousand if the disciples had hundreds of fishes and loaves, and just needed a little more? It was a great miracle because they had so little in their own hands with which to do what God had asked them to do.

When we are called by God to do a task, we often begin to look at what resources we have to perform it. This can be the beginning of our fall from the faith that will be required to do the true works of God. At the point we see our resources running out is when we will experience the power of God. What is needed to do the true works of God will not be found in our own resources or our own wisdom, but in the limitless resources of God.

We know that **"God is opposed to the proud, but gives grace to the humble" (James 4:6).** However, there is a false humility that is an offense to God and can keep us from being useful to Him. It was this kind of false humility that Moses displayed when God first called him at the burning bush (see Exodus 3).

When the Lord told Moses that He was sending him back to release His people from bondage, Moses responded by saying that he was not adequate for this great task. This seemed humble, but it caused the anger of the Lord to burn against Moses. The Lord was angry because this seeming humility was actually an ultimate form of pride and an affront to God. Moses was saying that his inadequacy was greater than God's adequacy. He was focusing on himself instead of the Lord. This is the one thing that may have caused more people to fail to fulfill their calling than any other single factor.

We will never be adequate within ourselves for what the Lord calls us to do. In our flesh, which is our natural strength, we cannot accomplish one thing for the Lord. That is why Paul the apostle told the men of Athens that the Lord is not served by human hands (see Acts 17:25). Only the Spirit can begat that which is spirit. We are utterly dependent on the Lord to do His work. We will never be adequate within ourselves for His work, and if we ever start to feel adequate we will almost certainly be in the midst of a fall from grace.

True faith is not a feeling of adequacy in ourselves, but rather of our focus on the adequacy of God. True faith is not a faith in our faith, but a faith in Him. The greatest faith is that which can see and believe in His provision in the time of the most pressing need. We need to see every circumstance that is beyond ourselves as an opportunity to see a miracle. If we are faithful in the little opportunities, He will bless us with greater ones. And yes, those blessings are trials.

We are about to see great miracles because He is going to allow us to come into places where we are going to need them. Let us determine now that we are not going to focus on the need or ourselves, but in Him. Let us prepare for these opportunities by focusing on Him today.

Take care, brethren, lest there should be in any one of you an evil, unbelieving heart, in falling away from the living God.

But encourage one another day after day, as long as it is still called "Today," lest any one of you be hardened by the deceitfulness of sin.

For we have become partakers of Christ, if we hold fast the beginning of our assurance firm until the end;

while it is said, "Today if you hear His voice, do not harden your hearts, as when they provoked Me" (Hebrews 3:12-15).

DAY 35

The Place of Miracles

For the kingdom of God does not consist in words, but in power (I Corinthians 4:20).

When the Lord fed the thousands with just a few fish and loaves, this miracle was so great because so much was done with so little. The Lord receives more glory when we have less in our hands to do His works. One of the greatest hindrances to our seeing the miracles of God is when we have too much.

When the Lord calls us to do a task, we must resist looking to our resources for the ability to carry it out, but rather look to God's resources. Having much may actually hinder us from doing great things for Him. When the Lord set about to change the world, He did not start accumulating a large treasury for the task. He just looked for twelve men that He could anoint. Even the men that He chose were lacking in the natural gifts and abilities to carry out such a purpose. However, the Lord did not need their abilities; He only needed a few who would be willing vessels for the Holy Spirit.

Years ago the Lord said to me that money was my least valuable resource. It is a resource and has some value, but it is the least of what we need to carry out His purposes. We need the Holy Spirit. There are a couple of crucial factors about the Holy Spirit that we need to understand if we are going to be used by Him. These are highlighted in the very first mention of the Spirit in Genesis 1:2:

And the earth was formless and void, and darkness was over the surface of the deep; and the Spirit of God was moving over the surface of the waters.

Here we see that in the first mention of the Holy Spirit, He is *moving*. In almost every mention of Him in Scripture He is moving. In John 3:8 we are told, **"The wind blows where it wishes and you hear the sound of it, but do not know where it comes from and where it is going; so is everyone who is born of the Spirit."** Those who are born of the Spirit will also be moving. The Christian life is not static—it is always moving, flowing, and going somewhere. This is the nature of those who are born of the Spirit.

The second major factor we notice about the Spirit in Genesis is that He brought forth this glorious creation out of that which was formless and void. He still loves to do this. We do not have to be perfect for Him to use us. We can actually be over-organized and over-prepared for Him to be able to use us. The Lord is not against organization, but in our pitiful little human perspectives our organization is often the result of majoring on minors. We want to get things ready, but He wants to get us ready. Our readiness is not dependent on the material realm, but on a heart that loves, trusts, and obeys Him.

It was for this reason that the Lord of the universe was born in a stable—the most humble, unlikely place He could have chosen. The only way He could be found was by revelation. The same is still true of those things that are truly born of God. The Lord is not waiting until our building is big enough, or for us to have enough money in the bank, or even for us to get a certain degree. He is waiting for us to have faith in Him—not in ourselves, and not in our stuff, but in Him.

DAY 36

The Great Commission

And Jesus came up and spoke to them, saying, "All authority has been given to Me in heaven and on earth.

"Go therefore and make disciples of all the nations, baptizing them in the name of the Father and the Son and the Holy Spirit,

teaching them to observe all that I commanded you; and lo, I am with you always, even to the end of the age" **(Matthew 28:18-20).**

We have often confused the good news of our salvation through the cross with the message of the Great Commission. Of course this is included in the gospel, but the gospel is much more than personal salvation. The foundation of the Great Commission is that all authority has been given to Jesus, in *both heaven and earth*. The Great Commission is not just a proclamation of our salvation, but of His authority.

Of course, our redemption is so wonderful and the message of the love of God which is established by it is so profound that it is easy to understand why many have a difficult time seeing beyond it. However, if we are to fulfill the Great Commission we must see beyond it. We were not commanded to go into all of the world with the gospel of salvation, but with the **"gospel of the kingdom,"** as we read in Matthew 24:14:

"And this gospel of the kingdom shall be preached in the whole world for a witness to all the nations, and then the end shall come."

The **"gospel of the kingdom"** is the good news that Jesus is the King who sits above all rule, authority, and power. He can at anytime reveal to the whole world that He is the King by peeling back the heavens. However, until the time of His return, He is seeking to call those who so love God and His truth that they will live in His kingdom now, even though they are opposed by the whole world which still lies in the power of the evil one.

We first proclaim Him as our own King by submitting our lives to His leadership and dominion. Then we seek to proclaim the good news of how much more wonderful it is to live under His dominion rather than under the domain of this present evil age. However, our message will be hollow and empty unless we are in fact living under His dominion.

That is why the Great Commission was not just to make converts, but to make disciples, teaching them to observe "all" that He has commanded. The most important step in any journey is usually the first, but we must acknowledge that the first step is just the beginning. As wonderful as it is, when one is born again, they are still as far from their ultimate purpose as an infant is from being the President of the United States. I use this example of the President because a Christian is called to something much higher than that—which is ruling and reigning with Christ.

The author of the book of Hebrews laments that he cannot give his readers solid food, but can only give them milk because of their immaturity. Hebrews is one of the deepest theological books in the Bible, with few Christians even comprehending many of its teachings such as that about the Melchezedek priesthood, yet the author says that this book is only milk! (see Hebrews 5:11-14). Where does this leave us? How do we go on to maturity so that we can partake of solid food spiritually?

The Lord spoke something to me years ago that so jolted me that I have since been on a quest trying to understand it. The Lord said that many multi-level marketers understand kingdom principles better than the present leaders of the church. An important insight about this statement came to me recently from a friend of mine, who has been one of the most successful multi-level marketers. I asked him what he considered to be the secret of his success. He replied quickly that it was the fact that when someone entered their business they were immediately shown how far they could go. Also each step toward their goal was clearly defined so they always knew where they were in relation to their goal and what they needed to do next to go higher.

How many Christians can say that in relation to their purposes in Christ? How many even know the next step toward pressing on to maturity? In polls I have taken in our conferences, it seems that less than 5 percent of Christians even know what their own purpose in Christ is. This must be one of the great and tragic failures of the modern church.

When I had the prophetic experience that I wrote about in *The Final Quest,* I had to climb a mountain. Each level on that mountain represented a biblical truth. As I climbed higher, I received more authority to defeat the enemies who were attacking us, and I also began to see more of the glory of the Lord. Since that time I have sought the wisdom of the Lord as to how to best implement the climbing of that mountain into our ministry and our message.

It is for the reason of trying to impart this systematic spiritual progression that I am writing this kind of book. Even though it is a daily devotional, I think you can see a systematic progression in it. I am already writing the next one, which I believe can help show the way to an even higher realm on the mountain of the Lord. As Proverbs 4:18 declares, **"But the path of the righteous is like the light of dawn, that shines brighter and brighter until the full day."** The light that we walk in should be getting continually brighter.

DAY 37

The Path to Fulfillment

As we studied yesterday, the Great Commission is not just making converts, but making disciples. The word disciple means "student." It also means "disciplined one." Both apply to our lives in Christ.

When we come to the Lord we become a lifelong student. As we read in I Corinthians 2:10, "**...for the Spirit searches all things, even the depths of God.**" Because this is the Spirit's nature, if the Holy Spirit is leading us we too will always be searching to know the Lord deeper. We will be compelled to know His ways, not just His acts. True Christianity and shallowness are contradictory to each other.

Because the word "disciple" also means "a disciplined one," II Timothy 1:7 declares, **"For God has not given us a spirit of timidity, but of power and love and discipline."** Few think of discipline as a fruit or gift of the Spirit, but it is very basic to the nature of the Spirit that we have been given. If we live by the Spirit we will be a disciplined people. This denotes controlling ourselves with focus and purpose. That is why **"self-control"** is listed as a fruit of the Spirit (see Galatians 5:22-24).

I Timothy 4:7-8 says to **"...discipline yourself for the purpose of godliness; for bodily discipline is only of little profit, but godliness is profitable for all things, since it holds promise for the present life and also for the life to come."** Nothing of significance has most likely ever been accomplished without discipline. If we will discipline ourselves in Christ, we will accomplish things that will bear eternal fruit. If we want to do anything of significance we must seize and apply the great power that is released through discipline.

I have been told a few times by friends who have known me from childhood that they cannot understand how I ever accomplished the things that I have. I understand their perplexity. Many of them are smarter than I am and much more gifted, yet they languish in jobs they hate while I am doing the kind of things they dream about. Why? Though I was a failure in school and seemed destined to a life of failure, when I was born again I was given the gift of discipline. Something gripped me so that I knew there was nothing more important, or more fulfilling than getting to know the Lord. While others were out having fun, I stayed home and studied for years. To them it looked like I was wasting my life, but now it looks like they were the ones who were wasting their opportunity to do something significant.

It does not matter how old you are or how many years you may have wasted, it is not too late to change. All discipline will pay off. Our discipline in the Lord will bear eternal fruit. Many would begin to live lives of great fruitfulness and fulfillment if they just took the time they now spend in front of the television, and instead spend it in front of the throne of God, seeking to know Him, and giving themselves to His service.

The following verses can change lives from one of defeat and discouragement into powerful demonstrations of the kingdom of God. Read them. Ponder them. Pray over them. Obey them.

> **and you have forgotten the exhortation which is addressed to you as sons, "My son, do not regard lightly the discipline of the Lord, nor faint when you are reproved by Him;**
>
> **For those whom the Lord loves He disciplines, and He scourges every son whom He receives."**
>
> **It is for discipline that you endure; God deals with you as with sons; for what son is there whom his father does not discipline?**
>
> **But if you are without discipline, of which all have become partakers, then you are illegitimate children and not sons.**
>
> **Furthermore, we had earthly fathers to discipline us, and we respected them; shall we not much rather be subject to the Father of spirits, and live?**
>
> **For they disciplined us for a short time as seemed best to them, but He disciplines us for our good, that we may share His holiness.**
>
> **All discipline for the moment seems not to be joyful, but sorrowful; yet to those who have been trained by it, afterwards it yields the peaceful fruit of righteousness (Hebrews 12:5-11).**

Do not waste your trials. They are more precious than gold. As the Lord said in Revelation 3:19: **"Those whom I love, I reprove and discipline; be zealous therefore, and repent."**

Day 38

Possessing the Promises

And we desire that each one of you show the same diligence so as to realize the full assurance of hope until the end,

that you may not be sluggish, but imitators of those who through faith and patience inherit the promises (Hebrews 6:11-12).

I am thankful for the great emphasis that many ministries have put on faith over the last few decades. However, as the text above declares, it will take faith *and* patience to inherit the promises. Isn't it strange that we have this huge "faith movement," but why have we never heard of a "patience movement?"

It takes two wings for an eagle to fly. If an eagle tried to fly with just one wing he would only spin around in circles on the ground. The same is true of many people who are trying to soar spiritually on their faith, but have not added patience. These just keep going around in circles, getting more and more frustrated and kicking up a lot of dust. Any truth that we teach without the counter-balancing truth will lead us to frustration, not fulfillment. In the following Scriptures we read about Abraham, who is called the "father of faith" (see Romans 4:12):

In hope against hope he believed, in order that he might become a father of many nations, according to that which had been spoken, "So shall your descendants be."

And without becoming weak in faith he contemplated his own body, now as good as dead since he was about a hundred years old, and the deadness of Sarah's womb;

yet, with respect to the promise of God, he did not waver in unbelief, but grew strong in faith, giving glory to God,

and being fully assured that what He had promised, He was able also to perform.

Therefore also it was reckoned to him as righteousness (Romans 4:18-22).

True faith does not waver over time, but becomes stronger. Therefore, patience is the proof of whether one's faith is real or not.

I meet many discouraged Christians who feel that God gave them promises that have not been fulfilled. If any promise of God is not fulfilled, we can be sure that the entire fault is on our side, not His. He is always true to His Word.

So what is it that we could be doing wrong? In most cases it seems that we are confusing faith with an emotion, and not joining it with patience. There are conditions with every promise of God. If we are not seeing His promises fulfilled, it is because we are not meeting the conditions. Having faith is one condition—having patience is another. If we get discouraged with the passage of time while waiting for a promise to come to pass, then we do not have the true faith of God. True faith always gets stronger with the passage of time, not weaker.

Between the place where the children of Israel were given the promise of a Promised Land and the Promised Land itself, there was a wilderness that was the exact opposite of what they were promised. The wilderness proved whether they would trust God, or doubt Him. The same is almost always true when we are given a promise. There is often a wilderness to go through to get to the fulfillment of the promise that is the opposite of what we have been promised. It is in this place that we must choose either to believe God or give in to discouragement and self-pity.

Self-pity is one of the primary destroyers assigned to keep God's people from walking in their purposes. If we allow self-pity or discouragement into our lives, we will wander in useless circles just as the first generation of Israelites did who left Egypt. If we believe God, we will in due time attain the promise. If we believe God, we will even rejoice in the wilderness, being thankful to have been called by God.

But thanks be to God, who always leads us in His triumph in Christ, and manifests through us the sweet aroma of the knowledge of Him in every place (II Corinthians 2:14).

DAY 39

True Discipleship

As Steve Thompson related in one of our leadership team meetings, there have been scientific studies made which indicate that the way that we are born can affect our whole lives. One example that was given is a procedure developed called "drug them and tug them," which was to drug the mother and tug the baby out. That generation became the one that turned to drug use in mass. Drugs are used as an escape from the pains of life.

It seems that there has also been a parallel to this in the church. When the gospel of an "easy salvation" or an easy new birth began to be preached, Christians in mass seemed to become easily addicted to spiritual drugs or doctrines that make you feel good while escaping reality. This message of an easy salvation was basically "come to Jesus and He will save you from all of your problems," rather than the biblical gospel that we come to Him to be saved from our sins, and to enter a life of radical discipleship and self-sacrifice.

I was given a prophetic word more than twenty years ago that "the saved needed to get saved." This word continues to ring in my ears as I have watched a veritable meltdown of morality and integrity in the western church. The weakness of Christians to stand against temptation and deception continues to grow rapidly. There is something fundamentally wrong with what is generally happening in Christianity today. When something starts going fundamentally wrong, it is the result of a problem with the foundation. We need to reexamine the very foundations of our gospel message, and the method, or lack of one, that is being used to disciple those who are coming into the church.

Because of excesses in the past with shepherding and discipleship, many believers now have a knee jerk reaction just to these words. As I have studied those movements, trying to understand what went wrong, I do believe that the methods which were devised by them promoted weakness and immaturity in believers rather than maturity. I am certainly not proposing a return to them, but there is a true discipleship and desperate need for true shepherds who will lay down their lives for the sheep and not just try to use them for their own selfish gain.

The apostle Paul described the gospel that he preached in I Corinthians 2:1-5:

> **And when I came to you, brethren, I did not come with superiority of speech or of wisdom, proclaiming to you the testimony of God.**
>
> **For I determined to know nothing among you except Jesus Christ, and Him crucified.**
>
> **And I was with you in weakness and in fear and in much trembling.**
>
> **And my message and my preaching were not in persuasive words of wisdom, but in demonstration of the Spirit and of power,**
>
> **that your faith should not rest on the wisdom of men, but on the power of God.**

A question that we must ask is: Are people today really being converted by the cross at all? Are we merely converting them to our denominations, doctrines, and to us? Are we even converting them to shallow promises of an easier life and deliverance from their problems? Following Jesus will not deliver us from all our problems—it will even give us some of the biggest ones, possibly even calling for our life! He did not come to deliver us from our problems, but from ourselves. He did not come to change our circumstances—He came to change us! Jesus is not coming cap in hand begging men to "accept Him." He still calls men to come to Him the same way He called them when He walked this earth.

> **And He was saying to them all, "If anyone wishes to come after Me, let him deny himself, and take up his cross daily, and follow Me (Luke 9:23).**

When Jesus called His disciples, it was for total commitment. They had to be willing to leave everything to follow Him, and so do we. If He is not the Lord of all, then He is not our Lord at all. As Paul also wrote:

> **For the love of Christ controls us, having concluded this, that one died for all, therefore all died;**
>
> **and He died for all, that they who live should no longer live for themselves, but for Him who died and rose again on their behalf (II Corinthians 5:14-15).**

Nothing less than this is true discipleship as the Lord Jesus Himself made clear:

> **"Not everyone who says to Me, 'Lord, Lord' will enter the kingdom of heaven; but he who does the will of My Father who is in heaven.**
>
> **"Many will say to Me on that day, 'Lord, Lord did we not prophesy in Your name, and in Your name cast out demons, and in Your name perform many miracles?'**
>
> **"And then I will declare to them, 'I never knew you; depart from Me, you who practice lawlessness' (Matthew 7:21-23).**

When we modify the message of the cross in order to make it acceptable, we destroy the power of that message to truly save. There are many "gospels" being preached today that have made multitudes feel safe in a spiritual condition in which their eternal lives were in jeopardy. Those who preach such a diluted gospel—and who promote such an easy Christian life, may be the biggest stumbling blocks living today. As Paul said, **"For Christ did not send me to baptize, but to preach the gospel, not in cleverness of speech, that the cross of Christ should not be made void" (I Corinthians 1:17).**

Before we can preach the true message of the cross, we must be delivered from the fear of man, the compulsion to be accepted by men, or the motive of wanting to receive anything from them. As Paul declared in Galatians 1:10: **"If I were still trying to please men, I would not be a bond-servant of Christ."**

If we are to walk with Christ, we cannot be controlled by the fear of man or the compulsion to be accepted by men. If we are controlled by these fears and desires, we will not be bond-servants of Christ. We do not preach in order to please men, but to please God. Our goal must not be to get people to respond to our message, but to *the undiluted gospel of Jesus Christ*. Only when we walk in this way are we truly walking under His Lordship, and only then will our message be true.

DAY 40

Truth in Preaching

Yesterday we studied about how there has been a great perversion of the gospel in our times. The gospel has been changed from "Jesus came to save us from our sins" to "Jesus came to save us from our troubles." There is an eternal difference between the two.

The preaching of a gospel that implies the Lord came to deliver us from our troubles often compels us to wait until a person is in desperation before we share the good news with them. Jesus did not send circumstances to lead men to Himself; He sent the Holy Spirit to convict the world of sin. If a person must be in desperate personal circumstances before coming to the Lord, then their purpose for coming to the Lord will be their circumstances rather than the conviction of their sin by the Holy Spirit. Just as those who were called by the Lord when He walked the earth were not in desperation because of personal circumstances, neither should a person's circumstances determine whether they are ready for the gospel or not.

The power of the gospel is not external. Its effectiveness is not dependent on the circumstances we are in, but on the Holy Spirit. If the Spirit convicts someone of their sins, they will bow the knee to the cross regardless of how well or poorly they are doing. If He does not convict them of their sins and their desperate need for the cross, then they are coming to Christ on a wrong pretense and a wrong foundation.

Whatever is built upon a weak foundation will likewise be weak. Is this not a primary reason for the weakness of Christians today? Is this not why there is such a meltdown of morality and integrity among Christians today? Studies reveal that there is no discernable moral difference between Christians and non-Christians. When there is no moral difference between Christians and non-Christians, then somehow Christ Himself is not in the Christian's life.

Could this reveal why Peter was sent to the Jews and Paul was sent to the Gentiles? Peter, an unlearned fisherman, was an offense to the Jews to which he was sent. On the other hand, Paul, a "Pharisee of Pharisees" was an offense to the Gentiles to which he was sent. The only way that either of them could be successful in reaching those to whom they were called was to depend on the Holy Spirit. If the Holy

Spirit did not come, neither would anyone come to the Lord because of the messengers. All true messengers will be but "earthen vessels." It does not matter what the vessel looks like—what does matter is what is inside. When we have to spend too much time dressing up the vessel, it is because of the weakness of what is in the vessel.

In many schools of evangelism there is a philosophy imparted that we must try to identify with those to which we are called to preach the gospel. This has caused many evangelists and missionaries to become neutralized in their work, and I have witnessed this to be the case with many who are in the field. However, if we are to be truly effective, we should understand that the Lord will probably send us to those who we cannot identify with and who will not identify with us, just as He did with Peter and Paul. Therefore, they will not come to Jesus because of us, but because of Him! They will come because the Holy Spirit touched their lives, not us.

There is a place for studying customs and cultures for the sake of not being unnecessarily offensive to people. However, if many of the missionaries I had met spent as much time studying the Lord, the truth of His Word, and seeking the anointing of the Holy Spirit as they did studying cultures, they would certainly be reaching far more people with the true gospel.

I thank the Lord for all who are in the field devoting their lives to reaching people for the Lord. I have also met many who are doing what I consider to be true apostolic works. Even so, the very fabric of Christianity is being weakened by many, here and abroad, who are preaching a gospel of easy problem solving, or a pseudo philosophy of identificational sensitivity (This should not be confused with identificational repentance for national and cultural sins). If people do not come to Jesus because of the desperation of one thing—their sinfulness and desperate need for the forgiveness that can come from the cross of Jesus alone, then they have come by way of a **"different gospel" (Galatians 1:6)** and they have come to another god who is not the real Jesus.

But I am afraid, lest as the serpent deceived Eve by his craftiness, your minds should be led astray from the simplicity and purity of devotion to Christ (II Corinthians 11:3).

When Jesus is lifted up on the cross, He will draw all men to Himself. If we lift up any other message for the sake of leading people to salvation, we are preaching another gospel.

DAY 41

Witnessing to Principalities and Powers

> To me, the very least of all saints, this grace was given, to preach to the Gentiles the unfathomable riches of Christ,
>
> and to bring to light what is the administration of the mystery which for ages has been hidden in God, who created all things;
>
> in order that the manifold wisdom of God might now be made known through the church to the rulers and the authorities in the heavenly places (Ephesians 3:8-9).

How does the church make known the **"wisdom of God...to the rulers and authorities in the heavenly places?"** First, we must understand the boast that Satan maintains before the throne of God.

When the Lord was about to destroy Israel in the wilderness, Moses interceded by reminding the Lord that if He destroyed Israel now, the whole world would say that the Lord had the power to bring Israel out of Egypt but He did not have the power to bring them into the Promised Land (see Numbers 14:13-16). Satan maintains a similar accusation against God concerning the church. He maintains that the Lord can forgive us for our sins, but He does not have the power to deliver us from our sinful nature, which is, of course, the work of Satan. In this way he maintains that his evil power is stronger than the Lord's because he controls mankind, even the redeemed of mankind. However, as we are told in Ephesians 5:25-27:

> Husbands, love your wives, just as Christ also loved the church and gave Himself up for her;
>
> that He might sanctify her, having cleansed her by the washing of water with the word,
>
> that He might present to Himself the church in all her glory, having no spot or wrinkle or any such thing; but that she should be holy and blameless.

Before the end comes there will be a church that is a worthy bride for the Lamb of God. She will be without **"spot or wrinkle or any such**

thing...holy and blameless." She will be a testimony to the entire host of heaven for all time that truth is stronger than lies, and the goodness of the Lord will always ultimately triumph over evil.

The bride of the first Adam lived in a perfect world and yet she chose to sin. Before the end comes, the **"last Adam,"** (see I Corinthians 15:45) Christ, will have a bride who lives in the darkest of times, a most imperfect world, and yet chooses to obey God. She will follow the light and walk in truth, holy and blameless before her Lord. She loves the truth more than she loves this present world or the acceptance of this present world. Because of this, for all of the ages to come, she will be known as worthy to rule with the King of kings.

Whenever we choose to walk in the light, even when the whole world follows after darkness, we are a testimony to the power of the light. Whenever we do right, even when the whole world does wrong, we are a testimony of the power of right. That power will one day overcome all of the wrong on the earth.

In this age, the greatest testimony of the power of truth and light is that it is willing to suffer and even die rather than compromise truth and light. The testimony of those who know the truth and light will be to live for that which is eternal, not just for the temporary. The willingness to suffer for the sake of righteousness is the ultimate testimony that one has the ultimate devotion to righteousness. This witness is even marveled by the angels, who will one day cause all to bow the knee to truth, righteousness, and the grace of God—He is the Source of all truth and righteousness.

The High Calling of God

For by Him all things were created, both in the heavens and on earth, visible and invisible, whether thrones or dominions or rulers or authorities—all things have been created by Him and for Him (Colossians 1:16).

This Scripture makes it clear that we were created *by* the Son and *for* the Son. This is carried a little further in Romans 8:29:

For whom He foreknew, He also predestined to become conformed to the image of His Son, that He might be the first-born among many brethren.

By this we must ask one of the ultimate questions: Would Jesus have come to the earth if there had not been a fall? I think so, because as glorious as the redemption of the cross is, the Lord made it clear that He came to do more than just redeem the earth—He came to begin a new creation, which we become a part of after our redemption. Consider Ephesians 1:3-4:

Blessed be the God and Father of our Lord Jesus Christ, who has blessed us with every spiritual blessing in the heavenly places in Christ

just as He chose us in Him *before the foundation* of the world, that we should be holy and blameless before Him, in love.

We were known by the Lord **"before the foundation of the world,"** and He was crucified before the foundation of the world. The Lord knew the end from the beginning, and He knew that man would fall and require redemption. But there was also a higher purpose for man in God's heart before He created him. He obviously had the new creation in His heart as well as the redemption of the former one.

This new creation was the intention for man to ascend from the natural realm to the heavenly nature. Man was to be the bridge between the natural creation and the heavenly or spiritual realm.

Through the Holy Spirit we have this treasure in earthly vessels, but we are called to take on the nature of the spiritual realm. When we are born again by the Spirit we actually become a new species. We walk the earth, but by the Spirit we can now dwell in the heavenly places with Christ.

Even if there had not been a transgression, it was always the Lord's intention for man to partake of a heavenly calling and be united with Him in a special way through His Son. When we are born we are just beginning life; when we are born again we are just beginning the process of spiritual maturity. Our goal is to be like the Lord and do the works that He did. He was the firstborn of many brethren. He came to redeem us, but also to show us how to live in the new creation nature. That nature has authority over the things that were the result of the Fall, such as sickness and the host of hell that has inhabited the earth through the gate of hell opened by the Fall.

Again, this is in no way to belittle the glory of the redemption that we have through the cross, as it will always be the centerpiece of our very comprehension of the glory and nature of God. The cross is the only door through which we may enter the purposes of God. However, we must also realize that our purpose is more than just being forgiven of our sins, as great as that may be, or even to be returned to our intended state before the Fall, as glorious as that may be. Redemption is a gift of unfathomable value, but we must press on to the attaining of our ultimate purpose—to walk in the nature of the new creation. When we do, we will be walking as Jesus walked, which is the calling of every Christian.

DAY 43

The Great Ministry

Now all these things are from God, who reconciled us to Himself through Christ, and gave us the ministry of reconciliation,
namely, that God was in Christ reconciling the world to Himself, not counting their trespasses against them, and He has committed to us the word of reconciliation (II Corinthians 5:18-19).

The ministry of reconciliation is a ministry that is given to every Christian. Once we have been reconciled to God through the cross, it is our basic calling to help reconcile others to Him. The primary way that we do this is through the proof of a life that is reconciled to God. Just what does such a life look like?

The first thing that was lost by the fall of man was his relationship with God. Therefore, the first thing that should be restored by redemption is our relationship with God. The Lord created man for fellowship, and our primary purpose is to fellowship with Him. If there was a way to measure the degree to which redemption has worked in our lives, it would be by how close our relationship is with God. If we walk with God, we must become like Him as we are told in II Corinthians 3:18:

But we all, with unveiled face, beholding as in a mirror the glory of the Lord, are being transformed into the same image from glory to glory, just as from the Lord, the Spirit.

We cannot walk with God without beholding His glory. If we behold His glory, we will be transformed into His same image. We can therefore ask ourselves: Are we becoming more Christ-like? Are we growing in the fruit of the Spirit? Are we growing in the gifts of the Spirit? All the gifts are aspects of Him. Is this transformation noticeable to others? If so, they too will be compelled to be reconciled to God. When Jesus is lifted up, all men will be drawn to Him. If they are not being drawn to Him through us then we have somehow departed from the course.

This drawing to the Lord can be for Christians as well as non-Christians. There are many who have "come to Jesus," but all they ever received was a religion. The Lord did not save us so we could become members of a church. That is one of the benefits. True church life should be one of the most fulfilling things that we can do on this earth, but we must have an even greater vision than that. We do not serve God by serving the church; we serve God as members of the church. There is a difference. If we try to serve God by serving the church, it becomes an end in itself. As the Shulamite maid said to her beloved in the Song of Solomon 1:7:

> **"Tell me, O you whom my soul loves, where do you pasture your flock, where do you make it lie down at noon? For why should I be like one who veils herself beside the flocks of your companions?"**

When we are only content to be in someone else's flock, instead of developing our own relationships with Him, we veil ourselves. Then we will not be changed into His image, but rather someone else's image. This is why we are told that we must behold the Lord "with an unveiled face" (see II Corinthians 3:18) in order to be changed into His image. There are many veils Christians can put on that distort His image, causing them to be changed into a distorted image of Him. One of those veils can be the church itself.

We cannot be content to have a relationship with the Lord through anyone else or through the church. The Lord does not have any grandchildren. We are all first generation sons and daughters to Him. Ministers are friends of the Bridegroom who are called to help prepare the bride for Him.

When there is a spiritual intimacy between the Lord and His church, she will bear fruit and souls will be born into the kingdom. How would you feel if all of your children looked like your best friend? Why is it that so many Christians are conformed to the image of their church, denomination, or movement, rather than into the image of Christ Himself? It is because they are more focused on these than on Him. They are being changed into the image of what they are beholding.

When the church becomes what she is called to be, there will be nothing we want to do more in this world than go to church meetings. This is because we will be coming together to serve the Lord and to behold His glory. There is no one in the universe more interesting than God. Just as the highest calling of the priesthood in the Old Testament was to minister to the Lord, the highest calling that we can have is to minister to Him. Ministry to the people was a secondary calling. It is still important, but not as important as the ministry to the Lord.

If we do not draw near to Him we will have little more than a form of religion to minister to people. Our goal should be to stay so close to Him that His glory is reflected from us like it was Moses. People knew when Moses had been with the Lord. Do they know when we have been with Him? It should be said of us as it was the Lord's first century disciples in Acts 4:13:

Now as they observed the confidence of Peter and John, and understood that they were uneducated and untrained men, they were marveling, and began to recognize them as having been with Jesus.

When we have been with Jesus, we, too, will cause men to marvel. When the church gives her highest devotion to drawing near to the Lord again, she will be changed into His image, and the whole world will marvel.

DAY 44

The Beauty of Holiness

As obedient children, do not be conformed to the former lusts which were yours in your ignorance,
    but like the Holy One who called you, be holy yourselves also in all your behavior;
    because it is written, "You shall be holy, for I am holy" (I Peter 1:14-16).

Holiness has almost become a bad word among many Christians in our time. This is usually because it is associated with movements and teachings that are legalistic in their approach to holiness. Even so, not only is holiness fundamental to true Christianity, we are exhorted in Hebrews 12:14: **"Pursue peace with all men, and the sanctification without which no one will see the Lord."** Sanctification is a word that is often interchangeable with holiness, which means to be set apart, purified, etc. As this Scripture declares, we must be holy if we expect to see the Lord.

As mentioned, recent studies indicate that there is no longer a measurable difference between the morality of those who claim to be born again Christians and non-Christians. Christians, who are now sliding into debauchery so fast, when measured as a whole, soon will be less moral and have less integrity than unbelievers! What is even more shocking is that there are not alarms being sounded from every pulpit and meeting place in the land!

There are now grounds to justify calling Christians hypocrites. A hypocrite is someone who claims to believe or do one thing, but does another. Let us also not forget that Jesus Himself reserved His most fierce denunciations for hypocrites. If we are going to church and claiming to be Christians, but are doing the things that we know the Scriptures condemn, we are the ones that He was talking about. We are the ones who are bringing shame to His most glorious name.

However, the Lord is full of grace and mercy to those who humble themselves and repent of their iniquity. Even when King Ahab, one of Israel's most evil and idolatrous kings, repented near the end of his life, the Lord immediately responded to him with mercy (see I Kings 21:20-29). If we have been caught in the snares of evil, we must run to the Lord, not away from Him. He will have mercy and help us.

The Holy Spirit, who is the personification of the holiness of God by His very name, is also the Helper. God does not require us to do anything that He will not also empower us to do by His Holy Spirit. However, we must understand that this is His name for a reason. If we want the fullness of the Holy Spirit in our lives, we, too, must be holy.

The true key to living a holy life is not just determining that we are going to stop doing what we know is wrong, but to simply return to our first love, God. That is why the Lord summed up the entire Law of Moses with the two commandments: to love the Lord, and to love our neighbors. If we love God, we will not worship idols or do the things that offend Him because we are the temple of His Holy Spirit. If we love our neighbors, we will not murder, steal, or even envy them. If we live a life devoted to loving God and our neighbors, we will not do wrong things and will therefore fulfill the Law. True holiness is not motivated by fear, but love.

The true holiness to which the church is called is not a bride who is afraid that if she is not perfect her Bridegroom will punish her. True holiness is a bride who is so passionately in love with her Bridegroom that she wants to be perfect for Him in every way. Therefore, the first step in recovering any spiritual ground that we have lost by falling into sin is to pray for God to have mercy on us and restore to us our first love. To then stay on the path is a simple devotion of growing in love for Him and our neighbors.

DAY 45

Hesitating Between Opinions

And Elijah came near to all the people and said, "How long will you hesitate between two opinions? If the LORD is God, follow Him; but if Baal, follow him." But the people did not answer him a word (I Kings 18:21).

Our presidential election dilemma of 2000 seemed to be an accurate depiction of the spiritual state of the country. We were divided almost exactly right down the middle. Like the Mississippi River that divides the nation and continually drifts from one side to the other, public opinion is generally so centrist that the extremes on either side can push it a little to one side or the other. It will then resist the pressure and swing back toward the middle. Is this good or bad?

The economic interests of this country considered it a good thing. Wall Street leaders stated that their hope for the election was "continued gridlock in Washington." Wall Street was doing fine just the way things were, so they did not want the boat rocked in either direction. They prospered when one party controlled the White House and the other one controlled Congress. They liked the huge budget surpluses; they wanted them to keep piling up; and they did not want anyone to come with enough influence to start spending it.

For the moral interests of America, gridlock seems to be a bad thing, but is it? It can be either a great tragedy or a great opportunity. It will be a tragedy if the good people of this nation continue to sit back and wait for the government to do what they are called to do. It can be a great opportunity if the good people arise and take the moral and spiritual leadership that they are called to take.

My prayers will always be for the Lord to give us leaders who will stand for righteousness, truth, and justice. However, I do not believe that the destiny of this nation or any nation is found in its civil government, but in the church. Prayer can accomplish more than any election. One little prayer meeting can have more power than the United States Congress and United Nations Assembly combined. Prayer can move the hand of God in a way that no one can resist.

The world has been shocked by just how fragile the government of the greatest democracy in the world has proven to be. The whole nation voted, but it seemed for a while that it would be just a few people who lived in a single county or even a single local judge who would decide who would sit in the most powerful political office on earth. Circumstances set the stage so that when either one prevailed, one half of the nation would feel that they were cheated. That set the stage for one to potentially sit in the most powerful office in the world, without much power. Wall Street may have liked it for a while, but even their prosperity is based on the faith of the people in the system, and that faith was close to being seriously eroded. The result of this shaking was an economic decline.

It does seem that much of the remaining morality in America is based more on civic morality than a true faith in God and His standards. The stage is being set for the true heart of the nation to be revealed. We will not like what we see. Many who thought that they had been worshiping the true God will find that they have in fact only been worshiping the idols fashioned by our culture. We are in desperate need for the church to arise with the prophetic resolution of Elijah to stand for the one and only true God and have the power to demonstrate it. This is not the power of the vote, but the power of the Holy Spirit. As we are told in I Corinthians 4:20, **"For the kingdom of God does not consist in words, but in power."** Before the church will be released with this desperately needed power, we, too, must stop hesitating between all of the worldly opinions.

The Lord is not a republican or a democrat. He is not coming to take sides, but to take over. He is not going to come back because of the will of the people, but because of the will of the Father. The church in America does not need the ability to win votes, what we need is a return to our true Source of power. Then, as the great apostle declared in I Corinthians 2:4, we too will be able to say **"And my message and my preaching were not in persuasive words of wisdom, but in demonstration of the Spirit and of power."** We need the ability to supernaturally demonstrate His power to men so that all who worship other gods can come to clearly understand that He alone is the One True God.

My main concern is not the indecisiveness of the American people as much as it is the indecisiveness of the church in America. If the church in America had voted for moral truth rather than their idols and their pocketbooks, that election would not have even been close.

The last church that the Lord Himself warned about in the book of Revelation represents the last day church. **"I know your deeds, that you are neither cold nor hot; I would that you were cold or hot. 'So because you are lukewarm, and neither hot nor cold, I will spit you out of My mouth'" (Revelation 3:15-16).**

As a citizen I was concerned about the outcome of the election. I am thankful to be an American. I believe in voting and praying for my country, but I am far more concerned about the general lack of prophetic resolution on the part of the church in America. My first citizenship is to another kingdom, of which I have been made an ambassador. I am more concerned about those who are called to be a part of the "holy nation" than I am this nation. Even so, I know that when the church awakens from her own moral depravity and spiritual stupor, there will be a witness of the one and only true God. Then the "prophets of Baal" will be silenced.

DAY 46

Where Is Justice?

Because I have something of a prophetic reputation I am continually asked my opinion about current events. This is a serious problem because I can give my opinion and it is often related as being a prophecy even when I make it clear that it is an opinion and not a prophecy. I do not presume to know the Lord's perspective on everything or even many things that relate to current events. I used to take His silence as rejection, but now I feel that there may be a message in it.

The last time He would not speak to me on a matter that I earnestly sought Him about was regarding Y2K. For months I inquired of Him with no response. Finally, when He did speak to me about it, He merely said that He was not speaking about it because it was not going to be anything. That, of course, turned out to be exactly right.

I have learned that many things in my personal life that I can be consumed with usually turn out to be insignificant and therefore just a waste of my worries. I have also learned many things that capture the interest and concern of the world do not even cause a ripple in heaven. Usually it is for the same reason these matters turn out to be unimportant. Because of this, I try to pray every day to see with His eyes, hear with His ears, and understand with His heart. I do not claim to be anywhere close to this now, but I believe that this is the calling of every Christian, not just those who are called prophetically.

I also like to watch the news and follow politics and business because they can reveal the heart of the people that we are called to reach. However, it is crucial that we are able to separate what the people are saying from what God is saying. These two are often not only different, but in opposition to each other. Even so, we can be thankful for democracy, as it is obviously the best form of government on earth. We can have the most perfect form of government, but it will be no better than the men and women who are in it.

Democracy is supposed to be the rule of the people. In such a form of government there will always be dissent. But if those who are in dissent are the minority, they must work to be more convincing to take their position before they have their way. This is how it is supposed to work. The courts have an enormous authority to dictate the actual application of the laws passed by the majority of people. Many shrewd people who understand this try to dictate policy by setting legal precedents. Precedent law is one of the widest open doors for injustice that can tragically pervert justice and the will of the people. Even so, our system of justice usually does remarkably well considering that it is run by people. All people are fallible, even the best Christians.

We must understand that the practice of law is an art, not a science. One can be dead wrong but still win in court by being able to articulate a more persuasive argument or by seizing a technicality. Because it seems that the entire presidential election was really decided by the Supreme Court, what should be our response to this as Christians?

First, we must keep in mind that even the most perfect government of man will not be perfect. The United States is not the kingdom of God and will have its flaws until the King returns. Half of the people in America not only felt that their man lost the 2000 election, but that they were cheated out of it. We were thrust into a situation in which either way it was decided would not be fair to the other side. We were simply caught in that terrible place where perfect justice was humanly impossible. It is time that we wake up to the fact that we have always been there. Perfect justice and perfect government are not humanly possible. Even so, because I have traveled much of the world and have seen the alternatives with all of their flaws, I am profoundly thankful to be an American and to live in a democracy.

I was once astonished as I watched the former owner of the Washington Redskins football team make a statement after his team lost a playoff game by what the cameras clearly showed was a bad call by the officials. He said simply, "The world is not fair. We should not expect to be treated fairly." He then talked about how it was their job to come back next year and play well enough so that the game would not have to be decided by officials.

I was personally thankful for the outcome of the 2000 election, but I also know if the good people in this country do not determine that they are going to work hard enough next time so that the outcome is not in danger of being decided by the officials, we are likely to find ourselves in the same situation again. If we are not happy about the outcome of that election and feel that it was stolen from us by a bad call, let us not become bitter, let us determine to work harder next time.

Let us also realize that even the greatest works of man are fragile, but we have a kingdom that cannot be shaken. As Isaiah 33:22 states, **"For the LORD is our judge, the LORD is our lawgiver, the LORD is our king; He will save us."** Here we see that the Lord Himself will fulfill all three branches of government: the judicial **(judge)**, the legislative **(lawgiver)**, and the executive **(king).** He is not sitting in the heavens wringing His hands in worry over any election. He cannot lose—He always wins. He has also given us this great promise:

> **Now it will come about that in the last days, the mountain of the house of the LORD will be established as the chief of the mountains, and will be raised above the hills; and all the nations will stream to it.**
>
> **And many peoples will come and say, "Come, let us go up to the mountain of the LORD, to the house of the God of Jacob; that He may teach us concerning His ways, and that we may walk in His paths." For the law will go forth from Zion, and the word of the LORD from Jerusalem.**
>
> **And He will judge between the nations, and will render decisions for many peoples; and they will hammer their swords into plowshares, and their spears into pruning hooks. Nation will not lift up sword against nation, and never again will they learn war (Isaiah 2:2-4).**

DAY 47

Wake Up Grandfather!

As I look out my window I can see Grandfather Mountain. It was named that because it looks like a man lying on his back sleeping. That is the perception that many have of their grandfathers. I have heard it said a number of times by the those of grandparent age that they just could not sleep during the daytime until they reached that age. The older we get we probably do need more sleep, but spiritually it is the most important time of all to wake up. We are in our greatest time of need for the wisdom and leadership of our grandfathers and grandmothers.

First, I believe we need to have the wisdom to be "spiritual grandfathers and grandmothers." This was a mandate for the Levites under the Old Covenant. They were prepared for ministry in the tabernacle or temple from birth, and then performed this ministry from the age of thirty until they were fifty. Then they retired from ministry in the temple, but entered into what may have been their most fruitful years serving as elders. As elders they sat in the gates as judges, and they discipled the younger Levites who were preparing for service. Let's take a moment to ponder the wisdom of this system, and how the church could desperately need it today.

In I Corinthians 6:5 Paul wrote, **"I say this to your shame. Is it so, that there is not among you one wise man who will be able to decide between his brethren."** In the previous four verses he admonishes the Corinthians because they were called to judge angels, but could not even decide minor matters in this life. It seems that possibly the greatest cause of the shame that repeatedly comes upon the church in our time is because we lack elders who will take their authority as judges.

As we read in Psalm 89:14, **"Righteousness and justice are the foundation of Thy throne."** It is right to emphasize righteousness, but we will never be able to walk in the full authority to which we are called, representing the throne of the Lord, until we also give an equal emphasis to justice. Presently, the church is filled with unrighteous judgment. Because those who are called to be judges in the church have not taken their responsibility in this area, some have assumed the position of being a judge in the church without the calling from God.

Most of the people who I have heard referred to as spiritual fathers were in fact spiritual grandfathers. We tend to think of men as spiritual fathers when they are old, but like in the natural, most men become fathers when they are young. Almost all of the leaders of truly dynamic churches that are still on the cutting edge of advancement, and are involved in further church planting, are led by those who are under the age of fifty. There are exceptions, but not that many. Just as most men start becoming grandfathers at around the age of fifty, if we have done our job well, those we have raised up should be the most dynamic producers in the church by the time they get to that age. Why not let them take over then? Most likely, there is nowhere for them to go.

When I inquired of the Lord about how to start a movement that would not stop moving, His reply was that I must use the wisdom of the geese. Geese fly in "V" formation for aerodynamic reasons. The geese that draft behind the lead bird use 20-35 percent less energy than the lead bird. Therefore, the lead bird can only stay in the lead for a short period of time before it will need to let another bird take its place, or the whole flock will start slowing down as the lead bird tires. This is why most churches and movements start losing their momentum so quickly. We do not know how to change leaders gracefully. Neither do we have a place for those who move out of being the point man in a congregation or movement. This one thing bogs down the momentum of a huge portion of the church.

For the church to make a place for its true elders, we must also recover and fulfill the commandment to honor our fathers and mothers. This was the commandment that contained the promise **"that your days may be prolonged, and that it may go well with you on the land which the Lord your God gives you" (Deuteronomy 5:16).** Not doing this is why many churches and movements do not remain as a vibrant, relevant force in the earth. Most effectively die with the death of their founder, or before, as they become a bottleneck to future advancement. If we will learn to transfer responsibility in the right way and at the right time, our churches and movements will keep growing in strength and spiritual authority.

The last days of a person's life should be their best and most fruitful. To do this we must know the time to turn over the reins of the day-to-day ministry in the church, and give ourselves to a higher calling. Just as Paul the apostle wrote most of his letters near the end of his life, that is the time when the wine of wisdom is the best. As Alex Haley once said, "Every time an old person dies it is like a library burning down." We should not be letting any of the great saints pass until they have left us all that they have to give.

We should also make a place for the true elders of the church in teaching and training the youth and children. These are the most important ministries in any church. We will not be bearing fruit that remains unless we are imparting our vision and our values to the next generation. Like the patriarchs of Scripture, we should not depart until we have prophesied over the coming generation, imparting destiny and vision for their future. Those who attain the promises will also be those who esteem the prophetic blessing of their parents enough to do whatever it takes to get it.

DAY 48

Changed by the Glory

But we all, with unveiled face beholding as in a mirror the glory of the Lord, are being transformed into the same image from glory to glory, just as from the Lord, the Spirit (II Corinthians 3:18).

As this Scripture declares, we are changed as we behold the glory of the Lord. Almost every Christian knows this, but it is remarkable how many get it backward in practice. Instead of seeking to see His glory so that they can be changed, they think that they have to change in order to see His glory.

As we have observed previously, when Adam and Eve first sinned they took the course that is a natural reaction to sin—they tried to hide from God. They also tried to cover up their own nakedness exposed by the sin. When the Lord called them out, they tried to blame shift to put the responsibility for their own failure on someone else. This is also a natural reaction to sin—hide, and then when exposed, blame shift. This is the path to darkness and further corruption.

However, the way of escape from both sin and the consequences of sin is to resist doing what seems natural. We must learn to run to God instead of away from Him. We must also seek to take responsibility for the sin, and not try to blame someone else. The Lord will forgive our sins, but He does not forgive excuses. When we make excuses for our sins, it is obvious that we have not really repented of it. As we are told in Hebrews 4:16:

Let us therefore draw near with confidence to the throne of grace, that we may receive mercy and may find grace to help in time of need.

If you take the first two chapters of the Bible, and the last two, you have a complete story. Everything between those four chapters deals with one essential subject—redemption. The Lord is in the redemption business. He seeks to take every failure and turn it into a victory for us. That is why the failure of the first creation led to the establishment of a new creation that was even greater than the first, enabling man to partake of the heavenly nature through Christ. However, the way we do this is through the cross. We must die to all that we are in order to partake of the new and greater life. We die in order to live; we lay down our lives in order to be raised up.

That is why we must learn to boldly turn to the throne of grace when we stumble, instead of trying to hide or blame shift. We do not have to wait to become perfect in order to enter into His Presence, but rather entering into His Presence perfects us. In all things, even our sin and failures, we must learn to turn to the Lord and seek to behold His glory. Then we will be changed. When we behold His glory, we will begin to reflect His glory because we will be changed into His same image. This is our ultimate calling—to be like Him and do the works that He did.

When we think of seeing His glory, we think of everything from beautiful colors to some perception of His nature. The story about Moses when he asked to see His glory gives us some insight into what we will see when we behold His glory.

> **Then Moses said, "I pray Thee, show me Thy glory!"**
>
> **And He said, "I Myself will make all My goodness pass before you, and will proclaim the name of the LORD before you; and I will be gracious to whom I will be gracious, and will show compassion on whom I will show compassion."**
>
> **But He said, "You cannot see My face, for no man can see Me and live!"**
>
> **Then the LORD said, "Behold, there is a place by Me, and you shall stand there on the rock;**
>
> **and it will come about, while My glory is passing by, that I will put you in the cleft of the rock and cover you with My hand until I have passed by.**
>
> **"Then I will take My hand away and you shall see My back, but My face shall not be seen" (Exodus 33:18- 23).**

When Moses saw the Lord's back, what did he see? I believe he prophetically saw the stripes that were on His back. Remember, the Lord was crucified from the beginning. When He created the world, He knew that He would also have to suffer and even die for it, yet He continued. There is nothing else that will ever more fully reveal His glory. When we truly behold what He did for us, we will be changed.

DAY 49

Follow the Shaking

"When he puts forth all his own, he goes before them, and the sheep follow him because they know his voice (John 10:4).

And His voice shook the earth then, but now He has promised, saying, "Yet once more I will shake not only the earth, but also the heaven."

And this expression "Yet once more," denotes the removing of those things which can be shaken, as of created things, in order that those things which cannot be shaken may remain.

Therefore, since we receive a kingdom which cannot be shaken, let us show gratitude, by which we may offer to God an acceptable service with reverence and awe;

for our God is a consuming fire (Hebrews 12:26-29).

In the verses quoted above, we see first that the Lord's people know His voice, and because of this they follow Him. We might also deduct from this that we will be able to follow Him to the degree that we know His voice. We then see in the text from Hebrews that His voice shakes things. So if we are going to know His voice, we are also going to know some shaking.

In such an insecure world, stability is much to be desired. However, if we seek stability and security above the truth, we may have ease for a time, but we will drift further from the Lord. Where the Lord is speaking, shaking is going on. If we want to follow Him, we therefore need to learn not to seek security in the things of this world, which will all shake when He speaks. We must find our security only in the kingdom that cannot be shaken—the kingdom of God.

If we start to shake when the governments of this world shake, it only reveals the degree to which we have placed our trust in that which can be shaken. If we start to tremble when the stock market begins to shake, this reveals the degree to which we have placed our trust in the stock market instead of in the Lord. As the text in Hebrews reveals, everything that can be shaken will be shaken. This should not surprise us. Those who know the Lord's voice and are following Him should be accustomed to this shaking. How should we then relate to those things that are being shaken?

First, if we have built our lives on the kingdom that cannot be shaken, and our ground is firm when what is around us starts to shake, we are standing on solid ground so that we can pull others out of the quicksand. We were not saved just for ourselves. The Lord loves all men and desires for them to be saved. We must always reach out to those who are having troubles in order to help them. Every blessing, grace, and provision that we have is for the purpose of demonstrating the love of God that saved and provided for us.

In Revelation 11:15 we read, **"And the seventh angel sounded; and there arose loud voices in heaven, saying, "The kingdom of the world has become the kingdom of our Lord, and of His Christ; and He will reign forever and ever."** The Greek word that is translated **"has become"** seems to indicate a transformation. There are aspects of our government that I believe have been founded on kingdom principles, and these will remain after every shaking. Whenever any part of our government, economy, or culture drifts from its moorings to kingdom principles, the shaking that will ultimately come will be more drastic and destructive. Even so, that which was built properly will remain through any shaking.

I have appreciated and enjoyed the prosperity we have had for the last few years, but I have also tried to order my affairs not to depend on it. I have watched as the time of prosperity has continued, people start appreciating their jobs less. The devotion to excellence has begun to suffer. A recession may be one of the healthiest things that could happen to our economy at this time, and we are indeed primed for it.

Before becoming a professional pilot, I worked for several years as a carpenter. I loved that trade and was privileged to work with an old craftsman who built houses like Michelangelo painted. Once during a recession I remarked to him that I was concerned that many who were in our trade were about to lose their jobs. He looked at me with a scowl and replied, "No true carpenter has ever lost their job during a recession. A true carpenter will always have plenty of work." There is a profound truth to this. If we are doing everything that we do as unto the Lord, devoted to excellence and integrity, even in this shaky world we will be okay. However, even better than that, if we are following the Lamb wherever He goes, we, too, will say:

But thanks be to God, who always leads us in His triumph in Christ, and manifests through us the sweet aroma of the knowledge of Him in every place (II Corinthians 2:14).

Think about it. If we are following Him we will always know victory. And our victories will not just be triumphs, they will manifest the knowledge of Him. This is why we are here.

DAY 50

A Newer Beginning

When I originally began this writing, we were approaching the beginning of a new century and new millennium. As this kind of change only comes every one thousand years, if there was ever a time to think of new beginnings this seems like a good one.

I have been asked a few times lately what I think of New Year's resolutions. Since this seems to be on so many people's minds, let me address this first before going on to my main point. Ideally, I think every day should be new for a Christian, and that we should not need such occasions to vow to make needed changes. I also know that "ideals" work only for a tiny percentage of people and the rest of us usually need whatever help we can get from such things. I also believe that the Lord, in His abundant grace, allows and may even appreciate our attempts to do what is right (using whatever crutches we need), as long as we do not build laws or principles of worship to Him out of them.

Even so, the highest and ultimate purpose of every Christian should be to live by the power of the Holy Spirit, not human crutches. The cross is the power of God (see I Corinthians 1:18). The power to meet every human need or solve any human problem is found at the cross. Why should we seek power any place else?

On New Year's Eve, at precisely the changing of the century, it was exactly one hundred years since the event that many mark as the true beginning of the modern Pentecostal Renewal—the outpouring of the Holy Spirit in Topeka, Kansas. Now hundreds of millions of people have experienced the baptism of the Holy Spirit. The movement that this event sparked has been the fastest growing spiritual movement in history, and instead of diminishing, it accelerated as we approach this new millennium. However, there is something coming that will mark the beginning of an even greater advance of the gospel, giving it more substance, depth, and power—the filling of the Holy Spirit.

Of course, we are filled with the Holy Spirit when we receive the baptism of the Spirit, but while trying not to get entangled in semantic terms, to be baptized in something is to be immersed in it. The baptism in the Holy Spirit is such a powerful, life-changing experience that there has been a tendency to think that this is all we need. However, in the book of Acts, long after the Day of Pentecost and the outpouring of the Holy Spirit, we have examples of the apostles doing extraordinary works when they were **"filled with the Holy Spirit"** anew (see Acts 4:8,31; 13:9,52).

There is no question that the baptism in the Holy Spirit is an empowering that can radically change our lives and result in much more fruitfulness for the gospel. D.L. Moody claimed to have had only a few conversions through his ministry until he received the baptism in the Holy Spirit, which at that time many referred to as "a second grace." This was also clear in the book of Acts. The apostles were filled with the Spirit on the Day of Pentecost, but even after this profound and powerful change in their lives, they still had other experiences of being "filled with the Spirit." What is my point?

I once heard a famous Pentecostal minister say that if Pentecostals and Charismatics were indeed Spirit-filled people, "we have somehow sprung a leak!" Is this why we see that repeated "fillings" were needed in the book of Acts? Perhaps.

Suppose we really did esteem the Holy Spirit as the most valuable treasure we could ever possess on this earth. If we had a great deal of money to carry, but kept losing significant amounts of it, we would make every effort to find out where the hole was and close it. How much more should we be concerned about why we are not staying filled with the Holy Spirit? What are the things that cause us to drift from the manifest Presence of the Lord in our lives? Are their holes in our lives that could even be so large as to call them "gates of hell," enabling the forces of hell to rob us almost completely of our inheritance in Christ?

Of course, the primary things that are going to offend the Holy Spirit are the things that are unholy. When we think of unholy we usually think of sexual lusts and perversions first. Undoubtedly, these are offensive to God, and the Scriptures are clear that the wrath of God will come because of them. However, in Ephesians 4:30 we are exhorted, **"And do not grieve the Holy Spirit of God, by whom you were sealed for the day of redemption."** Then we are told specifically how not to grieve Him in the next two verses: **"Let all bitterness and wrath and anger and clamor and slander be put away from you, along with all malice. And be kind to one another, tender-hearted, forgiving each other, just as God in Christ also has forgiven you."**

God is love, and anything that is not done in love does grieve Him. Sexual sin is a sin because lust is the counter power to love. Sex was created for love, not love for sex. However, all of the counter powers to love, such as bitterness, wrath, anger, slander, and malice, grieve and offend the Holy Spirit.

If there is a resolution we could make for this coming New Year, let it be to be filled with the Holy Spirit, to walk in the Spirit, and do nothing that would offend the Spirit. My prayer for you is that the prayer of the apostle Paul would be fulfilled in your life:

> **that He would grant you, according to the riches of His glory, to be strengthened with power through His Spirit in the inner man;**
>
> **so that Christ may dwell in your hearts through faith; and that you, being rooted and grounded in love,**
>
> **may be able to comprehend with all the saints what is the breadth and length and height and depth,**
>
> **and to know the love of Christ which surpasses knowledge, that you may be filled up to all the fulness of God**
>
> **Now to Him who is able to do exceeding abundantly beyond all that we ask or think, according to the power that works within us (Ephesians 3:16-20).**

Before the end, there will be a people who walk and abide in the Spirit. Because they walk in love, they will be entrusted with unprecedented power. In this way the kingdom of God will be demonstrated as the counter power to all of the evil that perverts and destroys on earth. Ultimately this power will prevail so that even the lion will lie down next to the lamb, and no one will hurt anyone again. Why not now resolve that we are going to be a part of preparing the way for this great kingdom? It is at hand.